Horses Helping Humans Follow Jesus

*The Transformational Journey
from Brokenness to Blessing*

Van Fielden

Renown Publishing
www.renownpublishing.com

Horses Helping Humans Follow Jesus / Van Fielden
ISBN-13: 978-1-952602-85-6

Praise for *Horses Helping Humans Follow Jesus* by Van Fielden

Van Fielden has a gift for taking profound truths and making them accessible and relatable. This book is a wonderful example, blending biblical clarity with real-life experience in working with two of God's magnificent creations: people and horses. It's a ring of golden keys that can unlock spiritual vaults full of potential and promise for anyone—including those of us who have walked with Jesus a long time. You'll want to read it more than once and pass it along!

Steve Richardson, President
Pioneers USA, Orlando FL

I like how the book is laid out in that it can be used as a Bible study, other group study, or individual personal study. Weaving together the therapeutic giftedness of the equine with the human need for a connection with God gives important insight to building and achieving good relationships with other humans and, ultimately, our relationship with God. The personal stories were a relatable bonus!

Rose Ingram, PATH Certified Therapeutic Riding Instructor
Jake E's Riding Roundup, Kaufman TX

Horses Helping Humans Follow Jesus is amazing and right on. (I also love the questions.) The horses help build confidence, leadership, communication, and so much more. Working with horses can help with work ethic, identity, and processing emotions. It's for people that may struggle with traditional therapy. The horse is a magical animal that God has given to us to bring us help and build our relationship with God as well as to understand our own identity.

Michelle Steinmetz, Transformation and Life Coach
Hope Equine Healing, Greeley, CO

This book is just like a great ride on my favorite horse at the crack of dawn. It centered me, quieted me, and helped me to breath, find focus, and connect closer with my purpose and my Heavenly Father. Horses can be seen as angels in fur, creatures only God could so perfectly design for us to get closer with Him. The author here takes everything good which we can gain from a horse to help inspect our hearts [and] to ride with joy for the cross.

Megan Hill-McQueeney, President/COO
BraveHearts Therapeutic Riding, Harvard and Poplar Grove, IL

Van Fielden's practical approach in *Horses Helping Humans Follow Jesus* is both immensely pragmatic and deeply encouraging. While many may find joy in horses, Van helps us all find purpose in life. His leadership principles help shape your direction and trajectory, wherever life finds you. And the stories told on the pages of this piece paint a vivid picture, for people both inside and outside the equine world, of the beauty found in human flourishing.

Brandon Reed, Senior Pastor
Vista Church, Orlando, FL

To my grandchildren—
silver and gold are not the point,
but the riches I have I give to you.
Follow Jesus.

CONTENTS

Regenerative Life in Christ

What does a pastor do when he "retires"? For me, I bought the farm. Yes, I literally bought a farm in South Carolina so I could help my daughter and her husband, Bekah and Mark Maddox, with their nonprofit, Hearts in Harmony. We use equine-assisted therapy to strengthen at-risk children and youth, men and women in addiction recovery, veterans and first responders, and so many others. As a result, I find myself writing this book, writing curriculum for Hearts in Harmony, fixing up two farms (the Fielden farm and the Maddox farm), and renovating our first rental house. Isn't retirement grand?

My seventh-grade English teacher once told me, "You will never be a writer." I believed her most of my life, until I recently had an epiphany: I wasn't much of a writer in the seventh grade because I didn't have much to say. A lifetime later, things have changed.

The single person who most encouraged me to write was

Don Richardson. In the last fifteen years of his life, Don became my good friend. I came to know him as a spiritual father and devoted elder in my church. Decades earlier, I had studied his work in seminary. He was known as a missionary, statesman, author, and highly respected thought leader in the world of global missions.

Don Richardson shaped the way we understand modern missions by helping us to see the simple yet profound truths most of us were overlooking. His books *Peace Child*[1] and *Eternity in Their Hearts*[2] demonstrate how God has embedded the idea of redemption ("redemptive analogies") into every human culture.

Early on in his ministry, Don was called by God to share the gospel with the Sawi people of New Guinea. Don knew that they were a tribe of cannibals and headhunters, but he also knew that they needed an opportunity to hear the gospel in their own language and culture. Through a deeply embedded cultural practice known as "the peace child," Don was able to explain the gospel in a way unique to the Sawi. They embraced Christ as God's peace child, and their transformation saved them from tribal extinction.

Don impacted my life in many ways, but mostly he helped me to see what others were missing. He encouraged me to use the realities of everyday life to help people find and embrace a new, redemptive, and regenerative life in Christ.

In retirement, my aim is to become something of a regenerative farmer. I plan to partner with our cows, sheep, goats, donkeys, horses, and wildlife to regenerate our farm's topsoil, increase its biodiversity, and return our farm to its

God-intended vitality and strength.

As a church-planting pastor, I have spent the last forty-four years of my life being a regenerative pastor, creating environments where God's people flourished. I spent those years either fixing ministries that were profoundly broken or starting new ministries from scratch. I have loved being a regenerative pastor. My hope in the writing of this book is that I will encourage you to be fruitful and multiply, bringing new life into your world, as you become a regenerative follower of Jesus.

Why Horses?

You don't have to have a horse to follow Jesus, but it helps. Horses help humans in many ways. People who work with horses know that they are amazing animals. That said, the premise of this book—horses helping humans to follow Jesus—will seem odd to some, but it's what we do.

How can a horse, who can't read or understand the Gospels and who doesn't have the words to explain a relationship with God, help anyone to follow Jesus?

We have been created to partner with God, and we are uniquely shaped to partner with each other. God has called us to exercise our authority and responsibility as we partner with and rule over His creation. Our leadership flows from partnership, not control.

Horses were designed to make great partners with humans. It doesn't really matter what discipline the horse is being trained for: show jumping, racing, reining, dressage, barrel racing, roping, plowing, cutting cows, mounted patrol, rescue work. A well-trained horse can do amazing things.

We've known for a while now that horses also make great therapy animals. They are gifted with sensitivity, honesty, and an incredible amount of grace. They have a way of touching the heart of even the most troubled soul. More specifically, horses provide opportunities for people to learn and practice patience, self-awareness, boundaries, communication skills, self-control, good attitudes, trust, coping skills, critical thinking, follow-through, leadership, mindfulness, faith, empathy, mercy, coordination, and more.

Horses are drawn to partnership with humans they trust. For any relationship to work, human or equine, there must be trust. Because horses are prey animals, they do not trust quickly or without relationship. For a horse to trust you, you must demonstrate that you are safe—that you are a potential partner, not a predator.

Horses don't tolerate bad leadership, which means that if humans want to partner with horses, the humans must step up their game. Most breakdowns in relationship between horses and humans are on the human side. Providing leadership for a horse requires humans to change and grow. When they do, they find partnering with a horse to be a mutually beneficial collaboration, good for the human and good for the horse.

Horses know that the world is a scary place, yet they still strive for freedom and connection. Like humans, many horses have had to navigate trauma, abuse, and neglect in this broken world. They have had to learn to adapt quickly to their ever-changing, often harsh, surroundings. For horses to thrive in this broken world, God has given them relational skills that help them to pair well with humans. But do they also have what it takes to help humans?

THE HUMAN CONDITION

When Jesus diagnosed the human condition for His disciples, He said, "The hearts of these people are hardened, and their ears cannot hear, and they have closed their eyes— so their eyes cannot see, and their ears cannot hear, and their hearts cannot understand" (Matthew 13:15). From Jesus' perspective, this was the universal human condition. He diagnosed humanity as clueless and hard-hearted, the two areas where horses are uniquely gifted to help humans.

Why didn't Jesus say that evil was the problem? There are so many wicked, evil, mean, bad, and nasty things people do to hurt themselves and others—things like intentional cruelty, deception, betrayal, abuse, and social injustice—yet Jesus focused on something as seemingly benign as the condition of the human heart. We tend to think the Bible teaches that it's the *really big sins* that separate humanity from God. We are convinced that outright evil is the biggest issue.

Evil is a problem, for sure, but really big sins are not responsible for keeping us separated from God and others. They are all forgivable in Jesus. The main problem with humanity is that cluelessness and hard-heartedness, in tandem, keep people insulated and isolated from God.

Without a connection with God, there is no work of God. There is no hope for redemption.

Jesus went on to say that because of people's hard and clueless hearts, "they cannot turn to me and let me heal them" (Matthew 13:15). Human hearts are broken, clueless, and hardened. That's what keeps people from being healed and transformed.

Jesus sees the evil. He is not missing the obvious. He knows that our behavior is a problem, but He understands that our issues run deeper. In His diagnosis, Jesus saw humanity as incapable of self-correcting and self-healing. Behavior management is a good thing and has its place, but we will see that Jesus pointed to something deeper: heart management.

We connect with God through our hearts, not our behavior. The heart is the root; our behavior (good or bad) is the fruit. Let Jesus heal the root and you will be on your way to producing more and better fruit. Your cluelessness and hard-heartedness are blocking you from knowing God and finding life in Him. This is, in short, the mission of Christ.

HOW'S YOUR HEART?

With all this in mind, there is one question you must ask yourself before you try to accomplish anything of significance in the world. Before you become a friend, a neighbor, or a co-worker. Before you take a job, start a business, make a sale, or manage a project. Before you fall in love, find a life companion, and start a family. Before you try to influence others, teach, mentor, lead, or persuade. Before you move forward, you must ask yourself this question: *How's your heart?* In other words, how are you doing on the inside? What's driving you or holding you back? For me, over the course of fifty-plus years of serving God, this has become the most commonly asked question in my family, my church, and my life.

Many people misunderstand what I'm asking. They respond with how they are feeling. That's part of it, but there is so much more to this question. The *heart* includes everything on the inside—the mind, the will, the internal narrative (story), the fears, the perspectives, and the attitudes, as well as the emotions. From this one question, many follow-up questions flow:

- How are you feeling?
- What are you thinking?
- What are you telling yourself?
- How do you see your current situation?
- Are you being honest?
- Are you believing a lie or a half-truth?
- Are you fearful, anxious, or worried?
- Are you bitter?
- Is there unforgiveness buried in your heart?
- How's your ego?

David prayed, "Search me, O God, and know my heart; test me and know my anxious thoughts. Point out anything in me that offends you, and lead me along the path of everlasting life" (Psalm 139:23–24).

Jesus gave us a framework for self-evaluating our hearts, which we call the parable of the soils (Mark 4:3–20). A parable is a made-up story someone uses to make a point, and Jesus used this kind of story often. In the parable of the soils, He noted that when a farmer plants a garden, not all the soil is equally productive. A farmer, much like God, wants to invest his life in promoting new life, growth, and multiplication. The condition of our hearts, like the condition of soil, determines whether growth, multiplication, and new life will take place. Jesus suggested that this is the first and possibly the most important of His parables for us to understand (Mark 4:13–14).

So, how is your heart? Jesus gave four possible answers to consider: hard, shallow, mismanaged, or good.

The Hard Heart

Hard hearts develop because they're walked on or stomped on repeatedly. No one was born with a hard heart. It's something that happens over time. To self-protect, people close their hearts and form a hard, impenetrable shell around them. At some level, this works for them, but the damage turns out to be far worse than the benefits.

You hear and experience God with your heart! If your heart is hard, letting nothing in, you remain clueless, helpless, and without God. If your heart is ever to soften, you must first learn to protect it while keeping it open. Solomon wisely said, "Guard your heart above all else, for it determines the course of your life" (Proverbs 4:23). Jesus agreed. God wants to communicate from His heart to your heart. To that end, it's critical for you to start protecting your heart.

What can you do if you are hard-hearted? You can pray a twofold prayer:

1. God, help me to see what I'm not seeing.

2. God, please soften my heart.

This prayer works. It's helpful at every stage of your journey with Jesus. No matter how far you've come, hard-heartedness will try to work its way back into your life and perceptions. Pray and keep praying. God is exceptionally good at answering this prayer, at changing and healing the human heart.

The Shallow Heart

Shallow hearts look good on the surface, but on the inside, they are still as hard as a rock. If this is you, many people in your life may think that you have a healthy, receptive heart, but in reality, you have many significant unresolved issues you hide masterfully, deep inside. As a result, your faith doesn't seem to work. You try to reach out to God, but you can't seem to establish or maintain a connection. Your commitments don't stick. You repeatedly fall away.

Why? Because the roots of your faith need an open heart to thrive, not a hard heart disguised as an open heart. You're not just "a bit flaky," as some of your friends may think. No, it's worse than that. Your heart looks good from the outside, but it's profoundly broken. Unless you give your entire broken heart to God, there will never be long-term growth or productivity in your life.

You may even be fooling yourself and living in denial. You may think that looking good on the outside is all you need. If this is true of you, you're thinking like a Pharisee—the religious leaders of Jesus' day who prompted Him to tell this and many other stories. For now, ask yourself these questions:

- Why am I faking it?
- Why am I settling?
- What am I afraid of?
- Why am I content with less than God's highest and best for me?

It's time to find some answers.

The Mismanaged Heart

Instead of being hard-hearted or shallow-hearted, some people have hearts that are open but mismanaged. An open heart is good; a mismanaged heart is still ineffective. Most people would assume that an open, functioning heart is the end game. It's certainly better than a hard or shallow heart, but it's not enough.

An open, mismanaged heart is not being properly cared for. It's cluttered and distracted. Jesus pointed to things like greed, worry, out-of-bounds desires, and pride. He called them weeds that will suck the life out of the garden that is the human heart. If left unattended, they are the very things that will prevent new life, growth, and multiplication.

I once had a counseling student come to interview me for a class project. When we were done, I asked her why she wanted to be a counselor. She replied, "You know me. You know my story. You know how I've had issues with my birth father and my stepfather. It's taken me years to open my heart. I want to help other people with their damaged hearts so they, too, can have open hearts."

I asked what I thought was an obvious follow-up question: "To what end?"

She looked at me, somewhat puzzled, and said, "So people can have open hearts." As if I hadn't heard her the first time.

I asked her again, "But to what end?" She had no answer, so I told her Jesus' parable of the soils. I pointed out that an open heart by itself is not the goal. Certainly, we want to help people open their hearts, but for them to thrive, there's more work to be done.

Our hearts need to be decluttered. They need room for the Word of God to grow and multiply! Some of the people most antagonistic to Jesus were those with open but mismanaged hearts. Jesus said to them, "Yes, I realize that you are descendants of Abraham. And yet some of you are trying to kill me because there's no room in your hearts for my message" (John 8:37). This brings us to the final condition, the only viable option for our hearts.

The Good Heart

We say that someone has a good heart when that person means well, when we believe that the person's intentions are honorable or kind, or when we can see that someone is trying to do his or her best. Jesus meant something very different. Jesus was saying that the person with a good heart has an *undistracted* heart. An undistracted heart positions someone to be wholeheartedly devoted to God. A person with this type of heart lives an uncluttered and productive life.

In a good heart, the weeds have been pulled. The heart has been prepared and protected. The soil is ready, so the seed of God's Word takes root and then grows and grows and grows. As Jesus said, "The seed that fell on good soil represents those who hear and accept God's word and produce a harvest of thirty, sixty, or even a hundred times as much as had been planted!" (Mark 4:20). Those with good hearts flourish when they "hear and accept God's word."

When I was done explaining the parable of the soils to my young would-be-counselor friend, she said, "That's what I want." That day, she opened her heart wide to God. She began to set aside her distractions and follow Jesus. She heard and accepted God's Word. She went all in and began her journey of following Jesus. Today her family and her therapy practice in South Florida are both flourishing.

COMMUNICATE HEART TO HEART

When four men brought their paralyzed friend to see Jesus (Mark 2:1–12), Jesus *saw their hearts* of faith. In response, He turned to the man in the stretcher and told him that his sins were forgiven. The man was healed. How did Jesus know that the man's friends had hearts of faith? How did He read their hearts? Don't miss this: Jesus was constantly reading people's body language and behavior so He could know their hearts.

The house was packed. There was no room. There was no way to have a one-on-one audience with Jesus. Undaunted, these men climbed up on top of the house and somehow managed to lower their friend into the living room, right in front of Jesus. Their hearts were easy to read because their bold behavior declared their faith.

The people watching were not mad about the hole in the roof. They were not angry that the man was healed. They were shocked and furious that Jesus said He forgave the man's sins. Jesus asked, "Why do you question this in your hearts?" (Mark 2:8). How did He know that they were questioning Him in their hearts? Because their body language, facial expressions, and behavior revealed their unbelieving hearts.

Jesus spoke based on the hearts of His hearers. Go one step further: Jesus said what He said to open the hearts of His hearers. Jesus wasn't into shock value. He was working for heart change. But for many that day, their hearts were not ready. Some had hardened hearts. Others' hearts were crowded with weeds. But for those who opened their hearts to God in response to Jesus' words, there would be growth, multiplication, and new life.

ARE YOU AS SMART AS A HORSE?

Later, Jesus was in a synagogue and offended many people by healing a man's hand on the Sabbath. The Bible says, "He looked around at them angrily and was deeply saddened by their hard hearts" (Mark 3:5). He read their body language and behavior and was upset with the condition of their hearts. He knew what to say and do to get at their hearts. Jesus was amazing because He always communicated heart to heart.

But isn't behavior management easier? We may think that it's safer to call out bad behavior when we see it and then focus our time and energy on correcting it and establishing new patterns. What do you think? Are you as smart as a horse?

Horses communicate their hearts through their body language. They don't have to guess what the next horse is thinking. Their body language sends clear messages. So-called horse whisperers know this. Horses don't lie. They don't have words. They communicate heart to heart with body language and behavior. We, too, can do this if we are willing to learn from our equine partners.

Later in the Gospel of Mark, the Bible says that "Jesus

turned around and looked at his disciples, then reprimanded Peter. 'Get away from me, Satan!' he said. 'You are seeing things merely from a human point of view, not from God's'" (Mark 8:33). Once again, Jesus read the hearts of the disciples through their actions, and He knew that He had to correct Peter's errant thinking. Peter's heart and the hearts of the other disciples needed to hear Jesus' strong, clarifying words.

The Gospels repeatedly mention that Jesus looked at people before He spoke. For example, the Bible tells us in Mark 3:34, "Then he looked at those around him and said...." Isn't that an odd statement? Of course He would look at them! It's rude not to look at people when we're talking to them. Why does the Bible repeatedly include such an obvious observation? Because Jesus was reading people's hearts through their body language and behavior.

This concept of heart transformation before behavior management is the key to living your life in Jesus. This is the journey, not just the starting line. Think about it. What will happen when you experience the loss of a loved one or a setback in life? Your heart will want to harden again. The weeds of anxiety, unforgiveness, and bitterness will want to return and take over. Tending to your heart will always be a necessary part of your journey in Jesus.

Dealing with the heart is the foundation for true behavior management. God promised that He would do His part: "And I will give them singleness of heart and put a new spirit within them. I will take away their stony, stubborn heart and give them a tender, responsive heart" (Ezekiel 11:19). This is the covenant promise for all of us in Christ Jesus.

Horses communicate heart to heart. It's all they know. As a result, when we partner with them, they make great full-length mirrors to reflect our hearts back to us. When we are clueless and hard-hearted, they help us to see through our hard, shallow, and mismanaged hearts. Like I said before, you don't have to have a horse to follow Jesus, but it helps.

Chapter One Questions

Question: How do you see your current situation? What's driving or motivating you? What's holding you back? What lie or half-truth may be influencing your thoughts and feelings?

_____

_____

_____

_____

_____

_____

_____

_____

_____

Question: Are you fearful, anxious, or worried? Are you bitter? Is there unforgiveness buried in your heart? How's your ego?

_____

_____

_____

_____

_____

_____

_____

_____

_____

_____

Question: In what way do you think you're struggling most: a hard heart, a shallow heart, or a mismanaged heart? In what ways is your heart good soil for God's Word?

_____

_____

_____

_____

_____

_____

_____

_____

_____

_____

_____

_____

Action: Take the following steps to help make sure that your heart is good:

- Ask God to help you see what you're not seeing. Pray that He softens your heart where it has grown hard.

- Ask yourself in what ways you're faking it, settling, or fearful. Decide that you won't be content with less than God's best for you!

- Figure out what weeds need to be pulled from the soil of your heart (for example, greed, worry, out-of-bounds desires, or pride). Pray for wisdom and strength to pull those weeds!

Chapter One Notes

_____

_____

_____

_____

_____

_____

_____

_____

_____

_____

_____

_____

_____

_____

The Journey Begins

REAL STORIES
SKY AND AZI

When Sky first got out of the Marine Corps, adjusting to the civilian world was not happening at all. He had been injured. He was angry. He didn't want to be out. He had planned to be a Marine for the rest of his life. He resisted this detour. He didn't know how to function around civilians. After being around those rough, gruff dudes, he couldn't imagine going back to having a "normal" life.

After he got out, Sky was introduced to equine therapy. The first time around, he didn't realize the importance of building a relationship with the horse. He tried to dominate it and force it to submit to his will, just like in the Marine Corps. He barked out orders and expected them to be followed. If they weren't, he made it happen. That approach didn't go well with the horse. Sky was completely unsuccessful in completing any of the tasks assigned by his instructor. It was frustrating for everyone.

Then came a plot twist. Sky was given an opportunity to go overseas with the Free Burma Rangers, a multiethnic humanitarian service movement working to bring help, hope, and love to people in the conflict zones of Burma, Iraq, Sudan, and the Ukraine.

His new role was a significant shift from his past service. He had a new mission. He was there to serve as a medic on the front lines. To show God's love. To help, not to take out the enemy at all costs. God started to change Sky's heart, and he grew in his compassion for people.

When he returned home, Sky was given another opportunity for equine therapy, this time with a horse named Azi. Sky came equipped with a different perspective and awareness. He was looking for more of a relationship with Azi. Instead of freaking Azi out with his energy, Sky was more open to making some changes in himself so he could connect better with the horse. His new awareness set him up for success.

We asked Sky why he thought equine therapy was helping. Sky told us, "Traditional therapy doesn't work for many vets. We don't want to sit in a dark room and answer questions from people who don't understand what we've been through. A lot of guys have an issue with therapy today. They don't want to take pills and isolate because of their PTSD. This leads to an estimated seventeen veteran suicides per day and a host of other overwhelming issues. [3] What they need is a holistic approach of learning how to develop relationships with others in a healthy way.

"That's where equine therapy is different; it's hands on. The horses give us immediate feedback. They help us to grow and change. They help us to improve our relationship skills."

THE EPIC NARRATIVE

Our life journey is filled with unexpected twists and turns, potholes and ditches, heroes and villains, seasons of success and seasons of hardship. Your journey may appear random, but it isn't. The objectives of your journey were determined before time and creation. Your story is, in fact, a small part of a much grander, epic story. The Apostle Paul summarized this truth at the end of his life: "For God saved us and called us to live a holy life. He did this, not because we deserved it, but because that was his plan from before the beginning of time—to show us his grace through Christ Jesus" (2 Timothy 1:9).

To follow Jesus well, we need the backstory. We need to understand the lessons from the Old Testament story, the epic narrative of humanity's journey back to God. It paves the way for the introduction of our extraordinary hero, Jesus the Messiah. He is the larger-than-life hero, both exceptional and pure, courageous and empathetic. He demonstrated great strength and unwavering conviction. He was mysterious and, not surprisingly, misunderstood.

Our story also includes humanity as the damsel in distress. Romans 5:6 explains, "When we were utterly helpless, Christ came at just the right time and died for us sinners." Our hero's selfless mission was to make a way for humanity to journey back to God and, in doing so, become the people we were created to be. As Ephesians 2:10 tells us, "We are God's masterpiece. He has created us anew in Christ Jesus, so we can do the good things he planned for us long ago."

The single objective was stated in Adam and Eve's original mission from God and then echoed throughout the whole of the Bible: "Be fruitful and multiply. Fill the earth and govern it" (Genesis 1:28). This is to be accomplished through the blessing of God, which is made possible in His Son, our hero, Jesus.

Along the way, there are many plot twists, turns, ditches, detours, and distractions. There are impossible moments when all hope seems lost. But with each turn, we gain more clarity. Slowly, ever so slowly, we make progress. Ultimately, we find purpose, meaning, and transformation.

Each season of our story includes a lesson for the reader to learn. We are meant to be participants in this journey, not just spectators. Missing out on any one of these five lessons has the potential to get us off to a bad start or cause us to lose our way. The rest of this chapter provides a quick overview of each season and its corresponding lesson.

Where are you on your journey? As we begin, take a moment to assess on a scale of one to ten your own relationship with God in this season of your life.

1. Hard to explain

2. Distant

3. Broken down

4. Struggling

5. Going through the motions

6. Out of alignment

7. On the right path

8. Growing

9. Strong

10. Flourishing

Where are you on this scale today? Where do you want to be? With your answers in mind, let's take a look at the five lessons to be learned from our story.

Lesson One: Walk with God

Our first lesson is foundational to all the rest. We were not created to walk alone. Isolation is predictably our worst choice in life. On this journey, we are meant to walk with God and with each other. In the beginning, God walked with us in the garden in an unbroken relationship (Genesis 3:8–9). But with our sin, we were banished from the garden. Our relationship with God and His world was broken.

At that time, our response, which seemed to worsen with each generation, was to isolate ourselves from God, to go it alone and no longer walk with Him. Not a good move.

It isn't until chapter 4 of Genesis that we see signs of

humanity returning to God. It was rare at first, but it was happening: "At that time people first began to worship the LORD by name" (Genesis 4:26). They began to call out to Him. As far as we can tell, God's heart was wide open to their gesture. The Bible says of Enoch that he was "walking in close fellowship with God" (Genesis 5:24).

Similarly, "Noah was a righteous man, the only blameless person living on earth at the time, and he walked in close fellowship with God" (Genesis 6:9). As a result, God repeated to Noah what He had said in the beginning to Adam and Eve: "Be fruitful and multiply. Fill the earth" (Genesis 9:1). Like before, this was to be accomplished through the blessing of God.

This means that plan A is still on track. Being banished from the garden and relegated to this broken road of human existence is not God's plan B for us. It's a detour for sure, but the destination has not changed. God's purposes for us are still on track, and we accomplish them by walking with Him.

Back in the day, people walked together to get to a common destination. Today, we walk together to get to know each other better and share life with each other. For God, it's both.

We walk with God to fulfill His plans, but there is more to it than just walking toward a common destination. God wants to do life *with* us: "Come close to God, and God will come close to you" (James 4:8). And also, "the LORD has told you what is good, and this is what he requires of you: to do what is right, to love mercy, and to walk humbly with your God" (Micah 6:8).

Lesson Two: Partner with God

In chapter 12 of Genesis, the plot turned. God approached Abram (later known as Abraham) and invited him into a partnership: "The LORD had said to Abram, 'Leave your native country, your relatives, and your father's family, and go to the land that I will show you. I will make you into a great nation. I will bless you and make you famous, and you will be a blessing to others. I will bless those who bless you and curse those who treat you with contempt. All the families on earth will be blessed through you'" (Genesis 12:1–3).

Our partnership with God won't be an equal partnership, but it's a partnership nonetheless. In a partnership, both parties have responsibilities. For this to work, both God and Abraham had to commit to doing their part. Abraham walked with God by faith, and God blessed the world through him.

Our understanding of the purpose for our journey is expanding. We are beginning to see *what* God wants. He wants us to have a fruitful and productive shared journey with Him. We're also beginning to see *why* God wants it. He wants to bless the world through His partnership with us. That was and is the mission.

Why would God want to partner with humans? Yes, He could accomplish His purposes without us, but we can't flourish in this journey without Him. We were not designed to live our lives in isolation. Our ability to be fruitful and multiply doesn't work without His blessing in and on our lives. We need this partnership.

Partnership with God requires, first and foremost, our faith. Abraham's faith required vulnerability. God asked Abraham to leave everything he knew and trusted because vulnerability was a strong test of faith, and "it is impossible to please God without faith. Anyone who wants to come to him must believe that God exists and that he rewards those who sincerely seek him" (Hebrews 11:6).

In Genesis 15, God cemented the partnership with Abraham by establishing a once-and-for-all covenant with him based solely on God's faithfulness. The one thing God required of Abraham was faith.

In Genesis 22, Abraham received his ultimate test. Would he be willing to sacrifice his own son in obedience to God? Abraham passed the test. As a result, God promised, "And through your descendants all the nations of the earth will be blessed—all because you have obeyed me" (Genesis 22:18). For our faith to grow, we must be willing to be both vulnerable and obedient.

Lesson Three: See Life from God's Perspective

God is not looking for our opinion. He is looking for faith, obedience, and vulnerability.

Have you ever felt off track in your relationship with God? Have there been times when life didn't seem to make sense? Maybe you are feeling that way right now. If so, you are *not* lost. You are having a desert experience.

God used desert experiences, or detours, throughout

Scripture to accomplish His purposes in people's lives. Fast forward in our story to when Moses was fleeing for his life from Egypt. He was demoted to the life of a shepherd for forty years. This was a significant detour for someone called to liberate God's people and return them to their promised land.

After many twists, turns, impossible situations, and miracles, God enabled Moses and the Hebrew people to leave Egypt and pass through the Red Sea. As they reached the edge of the promised land, Moses sent out twelve spies to discern their next move. When they returned, ten said, "No, don't do it!" Two said, by faith, "Go for it!"

As a result, Moses and the people of Israel chose to disobey God and not go in. Unwilling to put themselves in a vulnerable position, they failed the faith and obedience test. Without faith, it was impossible for them to please God. As a consequence, God gave them a detour: forty years of wandering in the desert.

The Bible tells us that God took issue with the bad report given by the majority of the spies (Numbers 13:32). Both groups reported on what they saw. Both told the truth. What was the difference between the reports? The bad report was the result of the spies seeing life only from their human perspective and leaving God out of the mix. The good report was given by men who saw and interpreted their reality from God's perspective and made their decisions accordingly. The good report was directed and supported by hearts of faith.

The consequence of the Israelites' rejection of a season of vulnerability was forty years of vulnerability with God. Our comfort zone, where life goes our way, is not the place where we see the most growth. The people of Israel grew the most when they were in one of their many desert experiences.

All of this was designed to build their faith. They would learn to believe God, walk with God, and partner with God. This is why Moses told them, "Remember how the LORD your God led you through the wilderness for these forty years, humbling you and testing you to prove your character, and to find out whether or not you would obey his commands" (Deuteronomy 8:2).

Lesson Four: Never Arrive, Never Settle

As God's people, we are always on a journey with Him, even when we get where God is taking us. Life is a journey from beginning to end. The journey is not over until the end of the story.

When the people of Israel crossed over the Jordan River, entering the promised land, it must have been a time of nervous anticipation and expectation. As they entered, their instructions were clear: "Be strong and very courageous. Be careful to obey all the instructions Moses gave you. Do not deviate from them, turning either to the right or to the left. Then you will be successful in everything you do. Study this Book of Instruction continually. Meditate on it day and night so you will be sure to obey everything written in it. Only then will you prosper and succeed in all you do" (Joshua 1:7–8).

It is safe to assume that they didn't do well at being strong, courageous, or obedient. In a season when they should have been flourishing in God, their faith evaporated. They made it to the promised land only to wander away from God. Maybe they thought that they no longer needed Him. After all, they had arrived! As a result, "the Israelites did evil in the LORD's sight. They forgot about the LORD their God" (Judges 3:7). The biblical account later adds, "In those days Israel had no king; all the people did whatever seemed right in their own eyes" (Judges 17:6).

In their frustration, Israel wanted a king. They thought that a king would fix what was broken. God gave them clear instructions: "If this happens, be sure to select as king the man the LORD your God chooses. ... The king must not build up a large stable of horses for himself or send his people to Egypt to buy horses.... The king must not take many wives for himself, because they will turn his heart away from the LORD. And he must not accumulate large amounts of wealth in silver and gold for himself" (Deuteronomy 17:15–17). All of this came with an admonition to be faithful to God's word.

Being in the promised land should have led to prosperity, but instead it led to a royal train wreck. First was King Saul, who disobeyed God and rebelled against Him. The prophet Samuel announced to Saul, "Because you have rejected the command of the LORD, he has rejected you as king" (1 Samuel 15:23).

King Saul was replaced by King David. Of all the kings, David was the most faithful, but he wasn't perfect: "For David had done what was pleasing in the LORD's sight and had obeyed the LORD's commands throughout his life, except in the affair concerning Uriah the Hittite" (1 Kings 15:5). David's sins were forgiven, but they were not without consequences.

David's son Solomon started out his reign as the king known for wisdom. In the end, he chose the path of a fool: "He had 700 wives of royal birth and 300 concubines. And in fact, they did turn his heart away from the LORD" (1 Kings 11:3). Solomon violated all three commands for being Israel's king. He had too many wives (political power), too many horses (military power), and way too much gold (financial power).

Solomon's son King Rehoboam quickly crashed and burned: "But Rehoboam rejected the advice of the older men and instead asked the opinion of the young men who had grown up with him and were now his advisers" (1 Kings 12:8). And "when all Israel realized that the king had refused to listen to them, they responded, 'Down with the dynasty of David!'" (1 Kings 12:16). By the third generation of David's dynasty, his kingdom was divided into Israel and Judah. Israel walked away from God, and Judah struggled to stay the course.

Never arrive. Never settle.

Lesson Five: Transformation Through Adversity

No one chooses adversity as a change agent in life, but there is much to be gained from hardship. Adversity can cost us a great deal. It brings frustration, depression, sleepless nights, confusion, stress, pain, heartbreak, financial ruin, humiliation, loss of confidence, and more. But for those who endure, the ROI (return on investment) is stunning. If we let it, adversity has the potential to change us from the inside out. It regenerates our faith, trust, resilience, courage, strength, focus, clarity, vulnerability, humility, perspective, and intimacy with God.

Israel experienced its greatest seasons of growth not in its prosperity, but through adversity. Throughout its history, Israel's identity as the people of God was forged in the fire of adversity and persecution.

In this final season before the coming of the Messiah, God warned them that they must repent or else be overpowered and taken into Babylon for seventy years of captivity. The prophet Daniel was a part of that exile and experienced it from beginning to end. He served and flourished under four successive dynasties: Nebuchadnezzar and Belshazzar of Babylon, Darius the Mede, and Cyrus the Persian.

Through it all, Daniel was faithful, his influence consistent. He overcame the temptation to exchange his faith for a Babylonian lifestyle. He remained vulnerable yet still prospered under each iteration of Babylonian leadership culture. God saw Daniel through the days of a fiery furnace, the political maneuverings of his adversaries, and the reality of a lion's den.

In the end, when this season of adversity was completed, Judah returned to the promised land a stronger people. More devoted to God's Word. Poised and positioned for their coming Messiah. In Jesus, they would go on to the next level of walking with God, partnering with God, and living life from God's perspective. Jesus would ask only one thing of them: "Follow Me." Would they be ready? Are we?

THE STORY CONTINUES

Early retirement must have been indescribably difficult for Sky. Loneliness and isolation became his new secret enemies. His forced separation from his Marine brothers was particularly cruel. He was no longer considered "combat effective," no longer fit for his life mission.

Azi helped Sky to slow down. To breathe. To collect his thoughts and energy before he responded with words or actions. Equine therapy has helped Sky to see himself in a way that he wouldn't have otherwise.

In the past, Sky's strong personality dominated. He was willing to sacrifice relationships in order to accomplish his goals. With Azi's help, Sky has learned that it's not just about the mission. It's about how you get there. It's about how you interact with people.

Sky's journey is not over. Currently, as this book is being completed, Sky is in harm's way in Ukraine. His life still has its challenges. Some emotional turmoil and anger are still there. They show up in his face, stance, and posture.

Partnering with Azi has really helped Sky with his relationships and his ability to serve others. People aren't seeing Sky as a predator anymore but as a welcome partner. Learning these lessons has opened Sky to a new mission and a new, highly productive season of his journey.

Chapter Two Questions

Question: When it comes to living out your faith in God, in what areas do you find obedience easy? Where is obedience more challenging?

_____

_____

_____

_____

_____

_____

_____

_____

_____

_____

Question: How vulnerable are you? Are there specific ways or areas in which you struggle to trust God enough to be vulnerable with Him?

_____

_____

_____

_____

_____

_____

_____

_____

_____

_____

_____

Question: What is an example of how you have grown through adversity? If you are in a time of adversity right now, in what ways is it pushing you to grow?

_____

_____

_____

_____

_____

_____

_____

_____

_____

_____

_____

_____

Action: Where are you in your journey? Assess on a scale of one to ten your relationship with God in this season of your life.

1. Hard to explain

2. Distant

3. Broken down

4. Struggling

5. Going through the motions

6. Out of alignment

7. On the right path

8. Growing

9. Strong

10. Flourishing

Where on this scale do you want to be? What is the first specific step you will take in that direction?

Chapter Two Notes

Follow Jesus

REAL STORIES
SAVANNAH

I (Savannah) am twenty-six years old. I've been on and off drugs since high school. Over the past four years, my addiction grew out of control. During the Covid pandemic, it reached an all-time high. I was living in Arizona with my daughter and her father. I was so empty, so lost. I had no hope for my future.

I didn't know what else to do but use drugs, which enraged my child's father. One day, when he found out that I was at it again, he lost it. He became violent and busted my head open. He put me on a plane and sent me back home to Colorado with nothing but the clothes on my back.

I was discarded. I had lost everything. I had thrown it all away. My family. My daughter. My life. Everything. I was so broken that I wanted to die. Death seemed to be my only out, or so I thought. It's what I thought I wanted, but God had a plan for more.

Two weeks later, I put myself on a plane to South Carolina to a treatment center with a program that would attack my addiction. As part of a second program, Hearts in Harmony, I would work with horses to heal my very broken and messed-up heart. Slowly, slowly I began to change.

I found growth in community, people who were willing to open up and share their lives with me. I found family, people who were willing to wade into the mess with me. I found a mission, a purpose larger than myself. I found care for myself and for others. Those who, at some point in the past, had been weak themselves were now being strong for me in the hope that, one day, I would become strong and be able to help others.

I went from death to life. I couldn't have done it without God in my life. He did for me what I could not do for myself. I became a new creation in Jesus. As I write this, I am now eight months sober. I never thought I would make it this far. I was sure that I would die an addict. But here I am. I thank God every day for pulling me out of the pit of hell. He is so good!

FOLLOWING JESUS

Jesus distilled His whole message down to two words: "Follow Me" (Luke 9:23). He couldn't have made it simpler. It's what He said to the fishermen from Galilee who became His four core disciples. It's what He said to Matthew, a despised tax collector whom no one expected to follow Jesus. It was His open invitation to the multitudes attracted to His life and message. It was the last thing He said to Peter after the "Do you love me? ... Feed my sheep" conversation (John 21:15–17).

It's easy to hear but can be hard to do. How can we know that we are not just saying the right words and then falling short with our follow-through? Jesus warned that there will be those who finish the journey only to discover that they have not been walking in relationship with Him after all (Matthew 7:22–23). On the outside, their actions seem impressive, but on the inside, they miss Jesus altogether. Worse, they won't know that they have fallen short until it's too late.

Jesus said, "For my yoke is easy to bear, and the burden I give you is light" (Matthew 11:30). Jesus found deep personal joy in the simplicity of His message. He prayed, "O Father, Lord of heaven and earth, thank you for hiding these things from those who think themselves wise and clever, and for revealing them to the childlike" (Matthew 11:25). He also taught that "anyone [man or woman, boy or girl, rich or poor, sophisticated or simple] who listens to my teaching and follows it is wise, like a person who builds a house on solid rock" (Matthew 7:24).

Following Jesus is a journey, not a destination. Many who profess faith in Christ rest on the fact that they have arrived. They are now born again. They are Christians. As if there were nothing else to do. Following Jesus is not an accomplishment we make, but a lifelong journey we take. It's something we do and keep doing. If we walk with Jesus, if we live our lives the way Jesus lived His life, if we listen to Him, embrace His teaching, and apply it to our lives, we're following Him.

There are two nonnegotiable elements that must be present if we are truly following Jesus: (1) God's grace and (2) our faith. Everything starts there. The Apostle Paul said, "God saved you by his grace when you believed. And you can't take credit for this; it is a gift from God." (Ephesians 2:8). We didn't get to vote on how this would work. It's God's call, His decision, His invitation. These two essential elements, God's grace and our faith, are His requirements for those who want to walk with Jesus.

Grace is God's open heart to us, His undeserved love for us. It is not something we earn. It is His gift, flowing from His open heart.

Faith is our open heart toward God, our trust and belief in Him. It is the one thing He asks of us that pleases Him (Hebrews 11). Our faith flows from our open heart toward God.

BE TRANSFORMED

Paul said it best: "Don't copy the behavior and customs of this world, but let God transform you into a new person by changing the way you think" (Romans 12:2). This is seen throughout the history of God's people. We are not conformers, changing from the outside in. We are transformers, changing from the inside out. The presence of

God in our lives changes our hearts and minds in Christ Jesus.

There are two common mistakes in this regard. First, some people try to conform their way to God. This is a poor substitute for the transformational power of God found in Jesus. Second, some try to convert or conform others to the Christian lifestyle. Trying to conform our way to God changes very little. Following Jesus takes an inside-out transformation.

You know that you are following Jesus if your life bears the fruit of a transformed and transforming heart! That's how it works. In Jesus, your life is changed and forever changing. Paul said, "This same Good News that came to you is going out all over the world. It is bearing fruit everywhere by changing lives, just as it changed your lives from the day you first heard and understood the truth about God's wonderful grace" (Colossians 1:6).

Jesus said, "Yes, I am the vine; you are the branches. Those who remain in me, and I in them, will produce much fruit" (John 15:5). It's unavoidable. He also said that we would recognize those following Him "by their fruit, that is, by the way they act" (Matthew 7:16). If you are following Jesus, you should be able to see the fruit of a changed and ever-changing life.

There are four categories of fruit that result from your journey in Jesus. If you are following Jesus, you should be able to see all four kinds of fruit active in your life. The fruits we're looking for are growth, community, mission, and strength. If, at any point, you don't see these in your life, you are missing out.

Growth

We don't know much about Jesus' childhood, but we do know that "Jesus *grew* in wisdom and in stature and in favor with God and all the people" (Luke 2:52, emphasis mine). At twelve years old, Jesus was left behind at the temple because He was dedicated to His own growth.

If you are missing out on growth, you are most likely unwilling to take the first step. You are unwilling to repent. There is no growth without change and no change without repentance. This is not about following Jesus on our own terms. If we want to follow Him, we must be willing to let go of our own way of doing things and embrace transformation in Jesus. We must be willing to mature and become more and more like Jesus.

Jesus said, "You are to be perfect, even as your Father in heaven is perfect" (Matthew 5:48). You may find this command overwhelming and beyond reach. On the surface, it is. But that's because you are misunderstanding the word translated as *perfect*. It doesn't mean errorless perfection. It means that we are to become fully formed, mature, or complete. When we choose to repent and turn to Jesus, He begins a work in our hearts and lives: "The Lord—who is the Spirit—makes us more and more like him as we are changed into his glorious image" (2 Corinthians 3:18). It's time to grow up in Jesus.

Community

When the church began, "all the believers devoted themselves to the apostles' teaching [growth], and to fellowship [community]" (Acts 2:42). The word translated *fellowship* can be explained as a joint participation and shared life. [4] There is no one word or phrase that captures the full meaning. It implies intimate connection and community. [5] We can attend church every Sunday morning, drink coffee in the fellowship hall, join a small-group Bible study, or meet one on one with another believer and still not have shared life. The goal of all these activities is to create an environment where people can share their lives with each other and with God. Just showing up does not get the job done.

Jesus is looking for a deep, meaningful relationship with you: "I am the good shepherd; I know my own sheep, and they know me, just as my Father knows me and I know the Father" (John 10:14–15). God the Father and the Son know each other completely. Their level of openness is the model for our relationship with Jesus and each other.

Jesus clearly communicated His desire for an intimate, open-hearted relationship with everyone who follows Him. The sheep-and-shepherd metaphor helps us to see the level of love and devotion Jesus has for us, but there's more. Jesus also said, "Anyone who does the will of my Father in heaven is my brother and sister and mother!" (Matthew 12:50). We may be like sheep, but we are a family. We don't just serve God; we are part of His family in Jesus. As a family, we share life with God and with each other.

Mission

It is not hard to make the argument that Jesus was the most mission-led person who ever lived. Once Peter tried to get in the way of Christ's calling, and Jesus responded, "Get away from me, Satan! You are a dangerous trap to me. You are seeing things merely from a human point of view, not from God's" (Matthew 16:23). Peter was trying to protect Jesus from harm but had inadvertently attempted to dissuade Him from fulfilling His calling from God. Not good.

Jesus also said, "Don't believe me unless I carry out my Father's work" (John 10:37). For Jesus, His believability was found in His unwavering devotion to His calling. This calling was God's work for His life, and so it is with all who follow Him.

Jesus stated and restated His calling throughout His ministry: "For the Son of Man came to seek and save those who are lost" (Luke 19:10). He said, "I have come to call not those who think they are righteous, but those who know they are sinners" (Matthew 9:13). He also said, "My purpose is to give them a rich and satisfying life" (John 10:10).

If you choose to follow Jesus, His mission is now your mission. He said to all who would listen, "If any of you wants to be my follower, you must give up your own way, take up your cross daily, and follow me" (Luke 9:23). What does the cross symbolize? It is the tangible symbol of Christ's calling. It was His focal point in life and in death. You, too, must pick up your calling in Him each and every day.

The Apostle Paul, looking back over his lifetime of service, could verbalize his calling to his younger protégé, Timothy: "God chose me to be a preacher, an apostle, and a teacher of this Good News" (2 Timothy 1:11). If you don't understand your calling as clearly as Paul did his, start paying attention. Sometimes the best way to discern your calling is to look back over the years and identify the ways God has chosen to use you. Paul knew and lived his calling to the very end.

Strength

Jesus did not come to earth to live for Himself, but to be strong for the weak: "The Spirit of the LORD is upon me, for he has anointed me to bring Good News to the poor. He has sent me to proclaim that captives will be released, that the blind will see, that the oppressed will be set free" (Luke 4:18). The Spirit of God consistently gave Jesus the strength needed to complete His journey.

Throughout Scripture, we are directed to be strong for the weak: "Give justice to the poor and the orphan; uphold the rights of the oppressed and the destitute" (Psalm 82:3). Put another way, "pure and genuine religion in the sight of God the Father means caring for orphans and widows in their distress and refusing to let the world corrupt you" (James 1:27).

God's expectation that we have strength for others specifically includes providing for other Christ-followers in need: "If someone has enough money to live well and sees a brother or sister in need but shows no compassion—how can God's love be in that person? Dear children, let's not merely say that we love each other; let us show the truth by our actions" (1 John 3:17–18).

When we follow Jesus, we bear the fruit of the Holy Spirit's work and anointing in our lives. He makes us strong for the weak.

COUNT THE COST

Jesus also warned us, "Don't begin until you count the cost" (Luke 14:28). If you want to follow Jesus, if you want to live your life the way He lived His, it will come at a price. Are you ready to pay the price to pursue God's highest and best for your life?

If you are just starting, here are five questions for you to ask yourself to make sure that you are ready. If you have already begun your journey, perhaps you should take a moment to see if these questions point out any gaps in your commitment.

Are You Willing to *Live from Your Heart*?

You know this is your starting point. Solomon was clear when he advised, "Guard your heart above all else, for it determines the course of your life" (Proverbs 4:23). Jesus said, "God blesses those whose hearts are pure, for they will see God" (Matthew 5:8). We are called to experience God and make the most of our life journey. If you are willing to partner with God in managing your heart, it will change the trajectory of your life. It will reframe the way you interpret the world around you.

Are You Willing to *Shift Your Perceptions*?

Are you willing to see what you're not seeing? Jesus said, "The hearts of these people are hardened, and their ears cannot hear, and they have closed their eyes—so their eyes cannot see, and their ears cannot hear, and their hearts cannot understand, and they cannot turn to me and let me heal them" (Matthew 13:15). How sad. You are clueless because your perceptions are broken. They are distorted by your hard, unmanaged heart, and they keep you from seeing what you're not seeing. Even worse, your broken, twisted perceptions are keeping you from being healed. They are blinding you and undermining your motives.

Are You Willing to *Align Your Motives*?

Your motivations matter. Even if they don't matter to you, they matter to God. You may have the people in your life fooled, but God knows your motives. You may even be hiding your heart from yourself, but that is not in your best interest, because "people may be pure in their own eyes, but the LORD examines their motives" (Proverbs 16:2). There is no hiding our hearts from God: "But I, the LORD, search all hearts and examine secret motives" (Jeremiah 17:10).

Jesus cares about your motives. Unaddressed, they corrupt your journey: "And even when you ask, you don't get it because your motives are all wrong—you want only what will give you pleasure" (James 4:3). For your motives to be what God wants for you, your perceptions must be what God wants for you. To correct your perceptions, you must back up and manage your heart. This is the journey.

Are You Willing to *Position Yourself in Christ*?

People of faith don't do miracles; God does. You can position yourself to be used by God in the miraculous, but that's all you can do. Miracles are God's decision, not yours. The greatest miracle ever was the birth of Jesus Christ. Mary couldn't make it happen, but she did position herself in obedience to be used by God (Luke 1:38).

The outpouring of the Holy Spirit is another good example. A handful of true believers positioned themselves in obedience to God and were filled to overflowing with the Holy Spirit (Acts 2:1–4). If you are not positioning yourself for God to use you, you've missed something. You have a problem with your heart, perceptions, or motives.

Are You Willing to *Be Productive in Jesus*?

It's clear that God is calling you to live a productive life. The productivity God is looking for is Jesus flowing through us and producing God's good and perfect will.

If you are in Jesus, productivity is unavoidable. If you're not as productive as He wants you to be, check your heart. Your heart impacts your perceptions, which impact your motivations, which impact your positioning in Christ, which impacts your productivity. Your productivity, in turn, impacts your ability to walk with Christ.

Ecclesiastes 10:2 tells us that "a wise person chooses the right road" while "a fool takes the wrong one." Thankfully, God knows the way: "The LORD says, 'I will guide you along the best pathway for your life. I will advise you and watch over you'" (Psalm 32:8). In short, "the LORD directs our steps" (Proverbs 20:24). You will live an amazing life if you are willing to be productive in Jesus, and there will be a great reward at the end of your path. Your journey awaits!

THE STORY CONTINUES

Through Hearts in Harmony, horses helped Savannah to rediscover her own heart. They helped her to see what she was not seeing. They helped her to internalize all she was learning in her addiction recovery program. Horses create a great learning environment, but they don't create the change and transformation; Jesus does.

Savannah's real story is not over. Her journey in Jesus has just begun. She will now need to walk the same road we all must walk. For her to continue to be successful moving forward, she will need to dedicate herself to Jesus' priorities for her life: growth, community, mission, and strength.

Savannah will need to continue growing up in Jesus. She must keep sharing her life with God and others as she lives in community. She must answer God's call as she discovers and pursues God's purpose for her life. She must become strong for herself and for the weak.

Savannah was lost. Now she's been found in Jesus. But to stay faithful on this broken road, she will need to protect her heart. She needs to be guided by God's perspective. Her view of life, herself, and others needs to be guided not by her addictions, but by the voice of God.

Chapter Three Questions

Question: In what ways are you willing to live from your heart? In what ways do you struggle with this?

_____

_____

_____

_____

_____

_____

_____

_____

_____

_____

Question: In what ways have you shown willingness to shift your perceptions? In what areas are you reluctant to do so?

_____

_____

_____

_____

_____

_____

_____

_____

_____

_____

Question: In what ways have you realigned your motives to reflect your commitment to God? In what ways do you resist doing this?

_____

_____

_____

_____

_____

_____

_____

_____

_____

_____

_____

_____

Question: In what ways have you positioned yourself in Christ? In what ways are you trying to control how you're positioned based on what you think is best?

_____

_____

_____

_____

_____

_____

_____

_____

_____

_____

Question: In what ways are you willing to be productive in Jesus? In what ways do you keep yourself from being fully available for His purposes?

_____

_____

_____

_____

_____

_____

_____

_____

_____

_____

Action: Are you ready to pay the price to pursue God's highest and best for your life? What are the most significant gaps in your commitment, as revealed in your answers to the questions for this chapter?

For each gap you identified, find and memorize a Bible verse that encourages your commitment to pursue God's highest and best. Then ask God for strength to count the cost and to commit fully to Him and His best for you!

Chapter Three Notes

_____

_____

_____

_____

_____

_____

_____

_____

_____

_____

_____

_____

_____

_____

_____

_____

_____

_____

CHAPTER FOUR

The Eyes and Ears of Jesus

REAL STORIES
BEKAH
Cofounder of Dark Horse Horsemanship
and Hearts in Harmony

Punky Brewster and Laura Ingalls were my (Bekah's) role models growing up. They were two of the "good guys." Like me, they were young women who were independent, self-sufficient, and willful. They were out-of-the-box thinkers. They were forces of nature. They had promise and potential. They would make their world a better place. I could relate to that.

Like Punky and Laura, I wanted to be one of the good guys. As far back as I can remember, I have always had a heart for helping broken, disadvantaged people. I have also had an unexplainable affection for horses. I had no way of seeing how these two passions would intersect.

I grew up in church. Even as a very young child, I had a strong desire for God in my life. He was with me, and I was with Him. But then, as a young teenager, I was sexually molested by a trusted family friend from our church. In the confusion, I did not realize the profound shift in my journey. My heart and my life had been damaged. A growing numbness consumed me.

Keeping secrets, repressing memories, and mismanaging my broken heart began to take its toll. I made bad choices. I ran to God for forgiveness only to return to more bad choices. Then I ran back to God, followed by more bad choices. I was confused, adrift. I was no longer "good." God no longer seemed near.

Was I getting what I deserved? Somehow, I thought so. I had been victimized, and over time, I came to see myself as a victim. I was becoming an outsider by choice. In my heart, I wanted to be one of the good guys, but I was convinced I wasn't.

I found comfort and fulfillment in my horses. While I was finishing my equestrian management degree, I spent my final semester of college in England, studying with the British Horse Society. Something about being away from home brought back a flood of repressed memories. My attempt to live a secret double life came crashing down. It had failed.

In my heart, I was broken and hardening. I desperately wanted to be a good guy, but I believed that I had forfeited the right. I had chosen to accept Christ's gift of grace for me as a child. Now it was time for me to return and embrace that gift as an adult.

Here's what I discovered on my way back to God: I was not alone. Jesus came, lived, and died so human hearts (including mine) could and would be changed. Jesus' open invitation to "come and follow" changed everything.

Looking back, I hated those broken, lost years of my life. My memories now are like watching a movie about someone else's life. That was the broken, damaged me. By allowing my heart to harden, I had unintentionally become part of the problem, living as if there were no God. The fruit of my life dried up. I stopped growing spiritually. I wasn't sharing life with other believers. I was just living for myself.

In those days, I struggled with God's mission for my life. I still had a heart to care for others, but I was running on my own strength. I was burning out. Now I live my life in Jesus. My journey on the broken road has taught me to trust Him to redeem my broken past. What others intended for evil, God has used for good.

GOOD GUYS VS. BAD GUYS

My dad once told me that there are three things you cannot do: climb a fence leaning toward you, kiss a person leaning away from you, and help a clueless, hard-hearted person who doesn't want your help. Those people are next to impossible to help because they don't realize their need for help (they're clueless). Even if they do, they don't care (they're hard-hearted). However, there is a way in Jesus. It's what He does. He makes a way where there is no way.

Jesus wasn't exactly a motivational speaker. Quite the

opposite. At times, it's hard to tell if He was trying to encourage or discourage His hearers. Jesus had no interest in becoming a self-help guru. He did not come to give us His top ten self-help strategies. Our salvation is found in following Him, in finding and developing a relationship with Him, not in figuring out some life hacks to make things easier for us.

Jesus knew that life is not about our circumstances, the things that happen to us. It's about the people we become through our circumstances. It's not about what's happening on the outside, but about the transformation that is happening on the inside. Jesus didn't promote a "fake it till you make it" approach. He didn't take or make shortcuts for us. He only wants what's highest and best for us. He is not so concerned about where we are on our journey today as He is about where we're headed on our journey tomorrow.

There was a rich guy who ran up to Jesus (Mark 10:17–31). He was sharp, motivated, enthusiastic, and well dressed. He was a dedicated soul, a winner. He was focused. He had initiative, credibility, and respect. Every outward indicator pointed to him being a person of great success. We would expect Jesus to recruit him without hesitation as a first-round draft choice to be one of His disciples.

This man had worked hard to live right. He was likeable, respectful, and sincere. He had a strong reputation for being a good guy. Jesus instantly felt a connection with him. Like many of us, this man believed that behavior management was the key to being a good person. He asked Jesus, "Good Teacher, what must I do to inherit eternal life?" (Mark

10:17). In other words, he was asking, "Am I good enough?" In our culture, we have grown up with the haunting, unanswerable question: "How good is good enough?" Everyone watching this interaction would have guessed that this rich guy was more than good enough.

This man wanted to know if there was anything he could *do* to prove his goodness, so Jesus gave him an assignment. Notice that Jesus wasn't aiming at the rich guy's behavior. He was aiming at his heart. When Jesus looked into the man's heart, He apparently saw lots of weeds. He said to him, "There is still one thing you haven't done. ... Go and sell all your possessions and give the money to the poor, and you will have treasure in heaven. Then come, follow me" (Mark 10:21).

Jesus said that there was "one thing" the man needed to do, yet He mentioned three things: (1) liquidate your assets; (2) give to the poor; and (3) come, follow Me. The two pre-assignments were given to the rich guy so he could pursue the one real assignment of following Jesus.

If you're wondering, people *don't* have to give away all their money to follow Jesus. They *do* have to declutter their hearts. The man had a tangled heart filled with selfish ambition that he was unwilling to address. He wanted to be seen as a good guy on the outside without having a good, productive heart on the inside.

Following Jesus doesn't work that way. To follow Jesus, we must live from the heart. If we don't, we will never see life the way Jesus sees it. Our perceptions will be broken. Make no mistake. We all have one assignment: to follow Jesus. To be ready, we must manage our hearts, our eyes, and our ears well.

Back to the story. The man had no response. He left, unwilling to understand, unwilling to follow Jesus. His journey was over before it had begun. He didn't have a behavior problem; his behavior was exceptional. He had a heart problem, a perception problem. This man was unwilling to live like Jesus to follow Jesus. A common mistake.

On the outside, this guy looked good, but on the inside, Jesus found him lacking. He seemingly had no need for God's grace or his own faith. He had no use for God's growth, community, mission, or strength.

The man appeared to live a fruitful life, but the fruit God is looking for is generated by God's presence working in and through our lives. Despite all his good behavior, the man was nowhere close to entering the kingdom of God. He would need to go back to square one and start from the very beginning.

Jesus always lived to please His Father. He always listened and obeyed the Father. He was pre-decided, pre-surrendered, and pre-positioned to honor His Father. He didn't have to think about it. He had no mind of His own, no opinion that competed with the word or the will of God. He lived for an audience of One. Jesus lived life from God's perspective alone!

LOST, NOT BAD

It's time for us to focus on seeing life and humanity the way Jesus does. Most of us prefer to think that there are two kinds of people in the world: good guys and bad guys. Good guys are good because, by our standards, they are good enough. Bad guys are bad because in some way, shape, or form, they are not like the good guys. The rich guy wanted to see himself as a good guy. He wanted Jesus to see him as a good guy. But through this story, Jesus introduced a new model for us to use to see and hear people the way He does.

In Jesus' day, everyone knew that the good guys were the Pharisees and the Sadducees, the masters of good behavior. The bad guys were the tax collectors, the sinners, the Samaritans, and anyone else unwilling to follow the lead of the Pharisees and the Sadducees. Today, for us, there are so many groups to choose from. The vast majority of groups tend to see themselves as the good guys and everyone else as bad guys, as evil or second-class.

To see people as Jesus sees people, we must have the heart, eyes, and ears of Jesus. Jesus sees two kinds of people: people with hearts that don't work (whom we might be tempted to label as bad guys) and people with hearts that do work (whom we might be tempted to label as good guys). Just remember that Jesus does not use the "good guy versus bad guy" model, so neither should we.

During His time on the earth, Jesus mostly saw people with hard, clueless hearts and characterized them as lost, not bad. They had lost their way on the journey. Jesus was only interested in transforming lost people into found people: "For the Son of Man came to seek and save those who are lost" (Luke 19:10). Lost people are unable to find their own way. They need to follow Jesus. Maybe that's why Jesus can love His enemies so freely. He doesn't see them as evil or bad. He sees them as lost.

THE PRODIGAL STORY

Jesus told a parable about a father with two sons. We know it as the parable of the prodigal son. But in this story, there are two sons, not just one. On the surface, one appeared to be the "good son" and one appeared to be the "bad son." Both were lost; they just didn't know it. The great insight from this parable is that life is not about our circumstances, but about our hearts.

In the parable, the father represents God. The two sons represent the good guys and bad guys in life. In the story, Jesus made the older son look exceptionally good and the younger son disgustingly evil by the social standards of that day. The "good" son worked hard and did everything his father asked of him. On the other hand, the "bad" son thought that he knew best. He wanted to be in control of his own life. He wanted to take the wide, easy road to fun and fulfillment. He claimed his inheritance early, counting his father as dead to him. He left behind his network of trusted family and friends, his supportive relationships, and moved in with a bunch of really bad dudes.

His laundry list of shortsighted, self-focused, and naïve

choices landed him in a place far less appealing than where he started. He wasted his inheritance and potential, which is why we call him the prodigal son. *Prodigal* means wastefully extravagant. [6] That seems appropriate. If that's true, how did the other brother prove himself to be the real prodigal by the end of the story? Maybe because life is not about our circumstances. It's about the people we become through our circumstances.

In the story, there was a turning point. Jesus said, "When he [the younger son] finally came to his senses, he said to himself, 'At home even the hired servants have food enough to spare, and here I am dying of hunger! I will go home to my father and say, "Father, I have sinned against both heaven and you, and I am no longer worthy of being called your son. Please take me on as a hired servant."' So he returned home to his father" (Luke 15:17–20).

The younger son had a change of heart, which triggered a change in perspective. His new way of seeing life wasn't completely accurate, but it was moving in the right direction. It would be corrected once he got home. This is not the end of the story.

Our "good guy versus bad guy" perspective keeps us from hearing the story the way Jesus wanted it to be understood. Let's start again. There once was a good father with two hard-hearted sons. One worked very hard in isolation. He really didn't enjoy or want to spend time sharing life with his dad. Neither did his younger brother, who picked up and left.

The younger son had a moment of clarity. He began to see his life through new eyes. He came to his senses and started learning from his mistakes. He realized that isolation from his father was a bad idea. His plan was to become like his older brother, the supposedly good son, and work for their dad. This was another bad plan, but it positioned him to reconnect with his father, which was the father's plan.

When he arrived home, his father was eager to share his life with him and celebrated the opportunity. Without hesitation, the "bad son" accepted his father's gift of grace, his undeserved love, and they all lived happily ever after. Well, not quite.

The "good son" (from our perspective) chose to retain his hard heart. Did his father ignore his hard heart and embrace him anyway? After all, he was very hard-working. No. This son showed himself to be the true prodigal. He would waste his life disguised as the "good son."

In anger, he chose to see himself as the victim, which hardened his heart even more. When people see themselves as good guys and then don't get their way, they begin to characterize themselves as victims. People never improve their lives when they choose to see themselves as victims. It didn't work then, and it doesn't work now. Think about it. Jesus was victimized. They crucified Him on the cross without cause, yet He never saw Himself as a victim.

In the end, both sons were trying to control their lives in their own ways. They were also trying to control their father. In our brokenness, we are all controlling in our own ways. We need to stop. Our heavenly Father is in control, but notice that He is not controlling. Sin is controlling. Satan is controlling. God is *not* controlling. God is sovereign. He is in control without the need to be controlling. When we begin to see God as sovereign, as in control, we don't have to continue our controlling ways.

THE STORY CONTINUES

Most people who know Bekah would classify her as one of the good guys, but she knows that's not the point. She was lost, and now she's found. She was a prodigal, and now she has been openly received as a child of God. She gets to embrace other prodigals as they come to their senses and turn toward home.

She was damaged, broken, angry, disgusted with her past life, and filled with shame, sadness, and fear. Now she walks with God, changed and ever-changing. She knows that she doesn't have to be perfect, just walking in partnership with God. She's no longer lost, no longer a prodigal, no longer a victim. Seeing life from God's perspective and following His lead has changed and continues to change everything.

Chapter Four Questions

Question: How close are you to following Jesus (a) by grace and (b) by faith?

_____

_____

_____

_____

_____

_____

_____

_____

_____

_____

Question: Are you bearing fruit in your relationship with Jesus? Review Chapter Three and evaluate yourself in terms of (d) growth, (e) shared life, (f) mission, and (g) strength.

_____

_____

_____

_____

_____

_____

_____

_____

_____

_____

Question: Have you surrendered yourself to the wisdom of Jesus and the Spirit when it comes to (h) your heart, (i) your perceptions, (j) your motivations, (k) your positioning, (l) your productivity, (m) your direction, and (n) your destination?

_____

_____

_____

_____

_____

_____

_____

_____

_____

_____

_____

Action: Overall, on what area do you need to focus the most in your relationship with the Lord?

Ask God for wisdom to grow in this area. What is one specific thing you can begin doing each day to help strengthen this part of your relationship with Him?

Chapter Four Notes

_____

_____

_____

_____

_____

_____

_____

_____

_____

_____

_____

_____

_____

_____

_____

_____

Motivation

REAL STORIES
EMILY, JACK, BUDDY, AND ROCKY

Emily was a young teen when her mom died of complications due to severe obesity. Emily had been taking care of her mom's needs and had not attended school since the third grade. She was fifteen when her adoptive parents (her maternal grandparents) enrolled her in a therapeutic boarding school that provided weekly equine therapy.

Emily's childhood was a mix of unstable environments that led to sexual abuse, being bullied by her classmates, and being neglected by her family members. She was diagnosed with Major Depression, ADHD, and ODD. By the time she began working with the horses, she was seemingly very tough. She had become very focused on her own self-preservation and trusted no one. She was angry, defiant, argumentative, disrespectful, and dishonest, among other things. She was stuck in that state of self-preservation and hiding her great fear of rejection.

Emily worked with three different horses over the two-and-a-half years she was at this school. Jack, her first horse, was very good at appeasing people rather than being real with them. She says that working with him "helped her to recognize her own appeasing, passive-aggressive ways" and that she learned "ways to be more decisive and consistent" while working on accomplishing goals with him.

After her first year, she went back home to try living with her adoptive parents again. After only four months, she returned to the boarding school due to struggles relating to her peers at her new school and not getting along with her parents as well as they all hoped. She realized that she still had more to learn.

When Emily came back, the equine staff asked her to pick a new horse to work with to broaden her experience and learn even more. We can always count on God to set the students up with the right horses! She ended up with a horse named Buddy, who, like Emily, had been severely starved and neglected when he was young.

Jack had given her a large dose of grace without truth. Buddy would give her a dose of truth with less grace. Emily said, "Buddy was blunt and direct, and I sugarcoat things. He taught me to be direct and honest toward him and others. By being straightforward, I became more confident."

Over the years, Buddy had worked his way to the top of the herd and had become a dependable, trusted herd leader. Emily had to treat him with respect to gain his respect in return. She was inspired by his story and progress.

After about nine months, Emily started working with another horse to allow another student to learn from Buddy. This new horse, named Rocky, was very strong in his own confidence and imposed himself on people he felt threatened by. This was something else Emily could relate to. She had not yet learned how to balance her own new confidence with the inevitable times of insecurity she would feel around others.

To lead Rocky well, she needed to learn to harmonize grace and truth. "Rocky taught me a lot about balance with self-confidence—leading and not lording over others," she reported. Horses can teach us many things, but they are particularly amazing instructors when it comes to teaching grace and truth.

MORE LIKE JESUS

If you were limited to one way, and only one way, to be more like Jesus, what would it be? For an answer, I would look to the Apostle John, who saw himself as "the disciple Jesus loved" (John 13:23). No one has ever had a closer friendship with Jesus or has known Jesus better than John did. He believed that if he wrote down everything there was to know about Jesus, he would run out of room for all the books (John 21:25). And yet, he distilled everything he knew about Jesus down to two words: *grace* and *truth* (John 1:14, 17 NIV). Grace and truth inspired, guided, and empowered the countless small decisions Jesus made every day.

What would your best friend say that you are full of? What motivates you? What are the defining characteristics of your life? Jesus' life reflected His understanding of certain basic realities, which guided the words He would (or would not) say and the actions He would (or would not) take. For Jesus, everything He did flowed from the two realities of *grace* and *truth*. He was never controlling toward people, because He always led with grace and truth. He would not act or speak in a way that was opposed to either of those realities—no compromise, no exception.

Jesus expected that those who followed Him would have a leadership culture that was different from the world's. They would lead from a heart of grace and truth. He explained, "Whoever wants to be a leader among you must be your servant, and whoever wants to be first among you must become your slave. For even the Son of Man came not to be served but to serve others and to give his life as a ransom for many" (Matthew 20:26–28).

Jesus also said, "I have given you an example to follow. Do as I have done to you" (John 13:15). For our behavior to match Jesus', our motivations must match His as well. Most of us know that we're supposed to follow the example of Christ, but what specifically was Jesus talking about?

Jesus had just washed His disciples' feet. He had taken on the responsibility of the lowest servant. Jesus was leading with grace and truth and from a posture of servanthood. We need to address our own motivations if we are ever going to lead the way Jesus led, serve the way Jesus served, and live the way Jesus lived.

THE GOOD SAMARITAN

One day, Jesus was tested by a lawyer, an expert in the Law of Moses. The religious leader asked, "Teacher, what should I *do* to inherit eternal life?" (Luke 10:25, emphasis mine). Sound familiar? Jesus had been asked this question before. How would Jesus answer this time? Would He say, "Liquidate your assets, give to the poor, and follow Me"? Not this time. None of the above. Remember that the question was: "What must I *do*?"

Since this man was an expert in the Law, Jesus flipped the test and asked him to answer his own question. The lawyer said, "'You must love the LORD your God with all your heart, all your soul, all your strength, and all your mind.' And, 'Love your neighbor as yourself'" (Luke 10:27).

Way to go! This guy's answer was exactly the answer Jesus would have given. The lawyer must be close, very close to the kingdom of God and eternal life. But then Jesus instructed him to go and *do* it. It wasn't enough to know the right answer; he needed to live it. That's the hard part, isn't it? Without the right motivation, the right answer doesn't mean that you are close at all.

The lawyer had asked what he should do. Ironically, he didn't have to do anything. He had to *be* a child of God and stop trying to make himself look good.

It's an odd question. What must anyone do to inherit something? An inheritance is a gift. You shouldn't have to do anything for a gift. That would be manipulation. All he had to do was receive the gift. If he didn't receive the gift, he wouldn't inherit it. Most gifts are motivated by one thing: love.

Ask any religious person about his or her core motivation, and the answer should be love. Love for God and love for people. The lawyer and Jesus had several words for love to pick from. They picked *agape*, the word used to describe God's kind of love. It's the love we are to have for God and for others.

Paul said that this kind of love is "patient and kind" (1 Corinthians 13:4). He went on to say, "Love is not jealous or boastful or proud or rude. It does not demand its own way. It is not irritable, and it keeps no record of being wronged. It does not rejoice about injustice but rejoices whenever the truth wins out. Love never gives up, never loses faith, is always hopeful, and endures through every circumstance" (1 Corinthians 13:4–7). In short, there are two sides of love: grace (undeserved love) and truth.

Jesus told another made-up (but very true-to-life) story to help the religious expert see what he was not seeing. The lawyer needed to see that words were cheap. His motivations were all wrong. His version of "good" wasn't good enough. It wasn't coming from the heart. Jesus told him a shocking story. We call it the story of the good Samaritan (Luke 10:30–37). It's a story about exceptional love, full of grace and truth.

There was a man traveling a very dangerous road. Along the way, a band of mean and nasty men jumped him, beat him, took all his stuff, and left him for dead. Because they stripped him of his clothing, no one passing by could identify his country, culture, or station in life. No one would be able to know if he was rich or poor, Jew or Samaritan, "good guy" or "bad guy." His identity was erased.

In time, two wonderfully religious people passed by. The first was a priest. He was a high-ranking, affluent religious leader, a guy who was paid to be good. He could afford to help. He knew the Law and what he should do, even for a stranger, but he just passed by. The second was a Levite, a more modestly paid, middle-management, religious guy. He also knew the right thing to do and didn't do it. He could have done something. Neither religious person was motivated to help. No love. No grace. No truth.

Enter the Samaritan—not the good guy Jesus' audience was expecting. What would have been the emotional response to Jesus introducing a Samaritan as the hero? Not positive. The prejudice toward Samaritans ran deep. Once, to insult Jesus and erase His influence, people called Him a "Samaritan devil" (John 8:48). They were just being mean. No one at that time was okay with the Samaritans. No one, that is, except Jesus.

THE TWO SIDES OF LOVE

The Samaritan is the character Jesus injected into the story to represent His perspective and motivations. The Samaritan was motivated to do the right thing. He was willing to embrace the mess in the messiest of situations. He chose to be strong for the weak. Why? Because that's what Jesus would have done, and it's His story.

Jesus was motivated by love—more specifically, a love

shaped by grace and truth. Grace is about giving people love they don't deserve. The Samaritan in the story was motivated by grace to help. Truth also demanded a response. Helping the man was the right thing to do. The Samaritan had the means and the margin—that is, the available time, energy, and financial or material resources—to take the man to safety and provide for his recovery, so he did. He loved the stranger the same way anyone would want to be loved.

Did the Samaritan choose to be strong for the weak to fulfill the Law? No. He wasn't a Jew. Moses gave the Law, which apparently was not enough motivation in this situation. Jesus came to us full of grace and truth, which are the right motivations.

The vast majority of Jesus' teaching came straight out of the Old Testament. Very little was new until He said, "So now I am giving you a new commandment: Love each other. Just as I have loved you, you should love each other" (John 13:34). If loving God and loving each other are at the heart of Old Testament teaching—and they are—then what's new?

Our new commandment from Jesus raises the bar. We are now to love the way Jesus loves, which means that we love from an open and whole heart. It means that our perceptions are changed. We no longer see anyone as an enemy. We don't perceive people as good guys and bad guys, but simply as people who need the grace and truth of God.

Individually, each side of love, grace and truth, is a powerful motivator. Each helps us to make the most of our lives. But together, they make us exceptional. They make us more like Jesus. Most people naturally gravitate to one or the other. One without the other is strong, but harmonized together, they bring us God's highest and best.

Truth matters to Jesus. He said, "And you will know the truth, and the truth will set you free" (John 8:32). The Father was His source of truth. Jesus said, "I do nothing on my own but say only what the Father taught me" (John 8:28). His relationship with the Holy Spirit was marked by truth: "When the Spirit of truth comes, he will guide you into all truth" (John 16:13). In praying to the Father, Jesus said, "Make them holy by your truth; teach them your word, which is truth" (John 17:17). Truth matters.

Grace matters, too. Jesus' grace was amazing. People never saw it coming. Jesus was known for His unexpected, unpredictable love. Paul instructed us, "Be strong through the grace that God gives you in Christ Jesus" (2 Timothy 2:1). Paul also said, "Live a life filled with love, following the example of Christ" (Ephesians 5:2). Jesus loved without hesitation. John explained, "That is how we know we are living in him. Those who say they live in God should live their lives as Jesus did" (1 John 2:5–6). Jesus' love was automatic. It was pre-decided.

Peter reminded us to "love each other deeply with all your heart" (1 Peter 1:22). That's what Jesus would do. But how do we follow His example?

HARMONIZE GRACE AND TRUTH

Have you ever sung harmony? It's an art form. It happens when two or more people sing different notes that were designed to be sung together. Done right, it's a beautiful thing. Like musical notes, grace and truth are meant to be harmonized. They are two different motivations that, by themselves, might lead us to love in two different ways. Harmonized together, they lead us to God's highest and best.

Most of us tend to be motivated by one more than the other. None of us were born balanced in this regard. Are you more a grace person or a truth person? Grace people tend to be okay with negating the truth to protect their grace. Truth people feel justified in squashing their grace for the sake of upholding their truth. Jesus was able to be completely devoted to both without compromising either. For Him, grace always harmonized with truth.

As the song of each of our lives continues, we must be intentional in keeping the harmony beautiful. As any song unfolds, the harmonies change. Similarly, as we live to follow Jesus, the lead note will shift. Sometimes it will need to be grace. Sometimes it will need to be truth. Neither should ever drown out or overpower the other. Our motivation should always be grace and truth together.

Jesus' mission was grace and truth, and we are now His agents of grace and truth. Paul said, "But whatever I am now, it is all because God poured out his special favor on me—and not without results. For I have worked harder than any of the other apostles; yet it was not I but God who was working through me by his grace" (1 Corinthians 15:10).

Two questions to ask if you always want to keep grace and truth in harmony are:

1. Is it true?

2. Is it helpful?

Before we say or do anything, we need to be able to answer "yes" to both questions. In Jesus, we are commissioned to be part of the solution, not part of the problem. We should only build up, never tear down. Paul made this clear when he said, "But our authority builds you up; it doesn't tear you down" (2 Corinthians 10:8). In other words, "let everything you say be good and helpful, so that your words will be an encouragement to those who hear them" (Ephesians 4:29).

THE STORY CONTINUES

At the beginning of her story, Emily's heart had been stomped on. It had, understandably, hardened. As a result, she was depressed, distracted, troubled, and unable to regulate her emotions. She was frustrated and reactive. But Emily's heart has been changed and is forever changing. Learning to harmonize grace and truth had created a new trajectory for her heart and life.

Emily graduated from high school in 2018 and is currently serving as a logistics specialist in the U. S. Navy. She has made tremendous progress and gives much of the credit for her healing to God, her heavenly Father, and the experiential therapy she had with horses.

Like Emily, we can't start with our motivations. We need to start with our hearts. If we see a breakdown with our motivations, we need to back up and start at the beginning.

How's your heart right now, today? Is it hard or hardening? Is it open but cluttered? Is it wide open for God to do His work in your life?

If you are motivated to live a life of grace and truth, that's a good sign. Your heart is probably in a good place. If you're not yet full of grace and truth, let's keep checking. You need to back up and check your perceptions. Are you seeing life and people the way Jesus does? Are you seeing good guys and bad guys? Or do you see people as lost and needing to be found, as prodigals who need to be embraced?

Look for signs that there's something off in your heart and perceptions. Do you have a breakdown in your desire for growth, community, mission, and strength? Are you are settling for believing lies or half-truths, denying the truth, or minimizing the truth? Not good.

In conversations, are you invalidating, isolating, or escalating? Are you stuck in negative interpretation mode? That means you have heart work to do.

Do you forgive readily, or do you let bitterness take root? Are you defensive? Have you simply shut down? Are you resisting the idea that you need to offer forgiveness, or receive forgiveness, or that there's work for God to do in your heart? Remember:

"If we claim we have no sin, we are only fooling ourselves and not living in the truth. But if we confess our sins to him, he is faithful and just to forgive us our sins and to cleanse us from all wickedness. If we claim we have not sinned, we are calling God a liar and showing that his word has no place in our hearts." (1 John 1:8–10)

You need to open your heart to God and let Him do what He does best: changing and healing the human heart.

Chapter Five Questions

Question: Are you seeing life and people the way Jesus does? Whom do you think of as good guys or bad guys? Where do you see people as lost and needing to be found?

_____

_____

_____

_____

_____

_____

_____

_____

_____

_____

Question: In conversations, are you invalidating, isolating, or escalating? How can you consistently show grace while holding to the truth?

_____

_____

_____

_____

_____

_____

_____

_____

_____

_____

_____

Question: Are you struggling to forgive certain people? Are you stuck in negative interpretation mode because of past experiences or your circumstances? Do you simply shut down in certain situations? How can you open your heart more to God so He can change you from the inside out?

_____

_____

_____

_____

_____

_____

_____

_____

_____

_____

_____

_____

Action: Identify someone in your life whom you need to see differently, the way Jesus sees him or her. Then figure out three specific ways you will change how you speak or interact with that person to demonstrate a heart motivated by Jesus' love, full of grace and truth in harmony.

Chapter Five Notes

CHAPTER SIX

Partnership

REAL STORIES
SAMMY AND GENESIS

Genesis and Sammy have been two favorite lesson horses for the past decade. Genesis is a black Andalusian–Quarter Horse cross. Sammy is a chestnut Arabian–Quarter Horse cross. Both horses are great for teaching partnership, but the partnerships look very different because the horses are very different.

Sammy is hesitant to engage in partnership with humans but enjoys it once it's established. When interacting with others, Sammy is unpredictable and headstrong. He's not the most obedient horse. He's curious and questions almost everything. With other horses, he positions himself in the middle of the herd. He's the class clown, playful and mischievous.

Sammy loves participating in endurance rides. He's eager,

overeager, to run. In twenty-five-mile events, Sammy's job is easy. He gets to go, go, go. His human partner's job is to help him stay on course and let him run. Sammy loves it. In a fifty-mile event, his human's job is to give him some boundaries and restraint. Sammy's job is to trust the leadership so they can finish strong together.

Genesis, on the other hand, is the master of conserving energy. He doesn't want to move his feet if he doesn't have to. He's very self-confident. He's more independent than most horses. He has been the alpha horse of his herd for many years. None of the other horses push him around, yet he is not rude or pushy with people. Genesis has partnered with humans in many different environments: dressage, hunter paces, obstacle courses, trail rides, and lessons.

Two great horses. Two great partners. Both have taught many humans the essential lessons of partnership. Both flourish in partnership, but their partnerships with humans look different because they are so very different.

WHY PARTNERSHIP?

Partnership matters. We were created for partnership with God, with each other, and with our horses. Horses were also made for partnership.

Horses, like humans, partner for success. Regardless of what discipline the horse is being trained for—show jumping, dressage, racing, long-distance runs, barrel racing, roping, cutting cows, rescue, mounted patrol—the bulk of time and energy in training is spent helping the rider and his or her horse to position themselves for their best performance through partnership.

Horses are hardwired to partner with other horses for survival. Have you ever watched a herd run from danger? Like birds, horses have an increased level of mirroring neurons. They can move as one. Their safety is in their numbers. Their strength is in their unity.

Humans have a lot to learn when it comes to partnering with others, whether horses or humans. Humans often want to control their partners, not work with them or lead them. When we work with horses, we may think that controlling the relationship is our responsibility because we like to see ourselves as being in charge. We choose domination over partnership when, in reality, leadership flows from partnership. In our broken model, the strong quite naturally dominate the weak. We think that's how it should work.

Our need for partnership is by God's design. Solomon said, "Two people are better off than one, for they can help each other succeed" (Ecclesiastes 4:9). A true partnership does not require equal standing. It requires mutual trust and respect. The partners can be quite different in what they have to offer, but the role each plays is both significant and necessary.

For those who follow Jesus, it shouldn't be a surprise that our spiritual journey depends on partnership. We were made for partnership. God designed us to walk in partnership with Him and with other believers. Our partnership with God is imbalanced on so many levels. God brings infinitely more to the table than we do, but He still expects us to do our part.

Paul said of Titus, "If anyone asks about Titus, say that he is my partner who works with me to help you" (2 Corinthians 8:23). He said of Timothy, "He is our brother and God's co-worker in proclaiming the Good News of Christ" (1 Thessalonians 3:2). And he said of Apollos, "We are both God's workers" (1 Corinthians 3:9).

There would be no Church without God's commitment to partnership. We see church as a building where believers gather. God sees the Church as a beautiful network of partnerships.

We must be intentional in our partnership with God and His people. We need to position ourselves for partnership, and we need to be pre-decided. We need to be okay with the fact that our partnership with God will change us from the inside out. We need to position ourselves to hear and follow His voice.

Position Yourself

For partnership to work well, positioning matters. We must walk with God if we are to partner with God. We must stay close, positioning ourselves to share our lives with Him. When it comes to horses, both the horse and the rider must be positioned correctly to work together. In our partnership with God, we must be intentional about positioning ourselves in Him.

If you want to be a hero of the faith, position yourself in God. Partner with God. God used people like Abraham, Mary, and the Apostle Paul primarily because of their faith

(Hebrews 11). Dig deeper and you will see that He used them because of their faith *and* their obedience. Dig deeper still and you will realize that the heroes of the faith all positioned themselves to be used by God. As a result, God could do the miraculous through them. If we're not willing to position ourselves, how can we expect God to use us?

Consider how many of the miraculous stories in the Bible happened because ordinary people positioned themselves to be used by God. Noah and the ark (Genesis 6–8). Abraham moving to the promised land (Genesis 12). Joshua at the battle of Jericho (Joshua 6). Mary offering herself to be the mother of the Messiah (Luke 1). Again and again throughout the pages of Scripture, people like you and me saw God move with indescribable power because they positioned themselves in faith, obedience, and vulnerability.

We cannot manipulate God. We cannot force His hand. We cannot obligate God to act. God is inviting us to partner with Him and play our part in the mission of Jesus. In our partnership with God, He leads, and we follow. In ourselves, we cannot create a miracle. The best we can do, through faith and obedience, is to position ourselves in Christ to be used by God. Then we watch Him move.

If you sometimes believe that other people get all the opportunities in life, then change your model. Position yourself for God's use. Do what we used to do in high school football. Don't just sit on the sidelines and watch. Be ready. Every time something goes wrong on the field and there's an opportunity for you to go into the game, be on your feet and say, "Put me in, coach! Put me in!"

We can't make God pick us, but we can be ready when He does. Stop sitting on the bench! If you want an opportunity for advancement at work, you proactively prepare and position yourself for that opportunity. Position yourself for partnership with God.

Way too many people think that they are people of faith because they believe in Jesus. The devil, too, believes in Jesus, and he trembles (James 2:19). Some think that they are people of faith because they never do anything wrong. Maybe it's more about what we're doing *right* in partnership with Jesus. True holiness is not passive. It's active. Holiness is about positioning ourselves, even with our imperfections, to be used by God for His purposes. It's time we all get a "put me in, coach" attitude!

Be Pre-Decided

To partner with Jesus, we also need to be *pre-decided*. We don't typically use this language, but we can understand the concept. And it's essential.

For example, on your wedding day, you will gather all your family and friends together to hear your long list of pre-decisions. You will read them out loud. These vows will be the most important part of the ceremony. You will pre-decide to love, honor, and cherish each other. Those decisions will be made before the marriage even starts. They will not be up for debate.

When a child is adopted, the parents tell the judge that they have pre-decided to love that child as their own for the rest of their days. When they have hard days as parents—and they will—they don't get to change their minds. They are pre-decided.

When high school graduates sign on the dotted line with the U. S. Marine Corps, they are pre-deciding. Whether they like it or not, whether they feel like it or not, when the orders come, they don't have to think about it. The correct answer is: "Sir, yes, sir!"

Jesus was pre-decided. We don't know much about His childhood, but we do know that He was pre-decided. He said to His parents after slipping away to the temple, "But why did you need to search? ... Didn't you know that I *must* be in my Father's house?" (Luke 2:49, emphasis mine). Why did He say "must"? At twelve, Jesus was already pre-decided about His commitment to God and the study of God's Word.

Jesus didn't use the word *must* lightly. When John the Baptist balked at baptizing Jesus, there was nothing for Jesus to decide. He was already all in. He said to John, "We *must* carry out all that God requires" (Matthew 3:15). When it came time to begin His ministry, Jesus was pre-decided. He declared, "I *must* preach the Good News of the Kingdom of God in other towns, too, because that is why I was sent" (Luke 4:43).

Jesus was pre-decided about His mission. At one point, Jesus called a timeout and said to Zacchaeus (the guy in the tree), "Quick, come down! I *must* be a guest in your home today" (Luke 19:5). Jesus was already on mission. Why stop and go in a new direction? Why did Jesus have to spend time with Zacchaeus? No one in the crowd that day liked him. But Jesus' mission was "to seek and save those who are lost" (Luke 19:10). Everyone knew that Zacchaeus was lost, but more importantly, Jesus knew that his heart was ready!

If we don't see Jesus as pre-decided, we are missing Jesus. We can see it in His language and behavior. We know from His prayer in the garden of Gethsemane that He was pre-decided to the very end. He prayed, "My Father! If it is possible, let this cup of suffering be taken away from me. Yet I want your will to be done, not mine" (Matthew 26:39). Jesus always did God's will, even when it would cost Him His life.

Be Different

Jesus said, "But among you it will be different" (Mark 10:43). Following Jesus changes the way we live our lives. It changes the people we become. We cannot partner with Jesus without becoming different people. Jesus said to Nicodemus, "So don't be surprised when I say, 'You *must* be born again'" (John 3:7). He wasn't asking Nicodemus to try harder at being good. He was saying that Nicodemus needed to become different from the inside out, which is the result of a spiritual rebirth.

Following Jesus makes us different in so many ways. Here's one. Peter was trying to figure out Jesus' take on forgiveness. He asked Jesus, "Lord, how often should I forgive someone who sins against me? Seven times?" (Matthew 18:21). How many of us struggle with positioning ourselves as people of forgiveness? Jesus blew him away when He replied, "No, not seven times ... but seventy times seven!" (Matthew 18:22).

When we balk at forgiveness, we balk at our pre-decision to be people of grace and truth. We cannot completely forgive without grace and truth, just as grace and truth cannot coexist without forgiveness.

Grace-only people want to forgive, but by minimizing or leaving out the truth. Are we really forgiving like Jesus if we are not being honest about the offense? An apology that doesn't own up to the offense is not much of an apology. The more honest and truthful the apology, the stronger the forgiveness.

Truth alone won't forgive, because truth-oriented people tend to believe that love must be earned and deserved. Forgiveness doesn't work that way. We do not forgive on a case-by-case basis. In Jesus, we forgive even when it's not earned or deserved. Even without an apology, we forgive completely because Jesus has forgiven us completely. As people of grace and truth, we position ourselves to forgive automatically. For those who follow Jesus, forgiveness is pre-decided. We don't need time to think about it.

Jesus has high expectations for us when it comes to forgiveness. He said, "If you forgive those who sin against you, your heavenly Father will forgive you. But if you refuse to forgive others, your Father will not forgive your sins" (Matthew 6:14–15). Did Jesus really say that? Yep.

Listen to God

Finally, for us to partner with God, we must position ourselves to hear the voice of God. Jesus had a strong habit of positioning Himself to hear God the Father. He even had a favorite place to go. Luke told us, "Then, accompanied by the disciples, Jesus left the upstairs room and went as usual to the Mount of Olives" (Luke 22:39). Jesus positioned Himself to hear His Father regularly. He stated, "I say only what I have heard from the one who sent me, and he is completely truthful" (John 8:26).

Over my years as a pastor, I have loved to take prayer walks. I learned a long time ago that I cannot make God speak, but I can put myself in a place to listen. If I take a walk with God and He doesn't speak, then I had a nice walk with God. If He does speak, His smallest word to me is significantly stronger and more helpful than my best idea on my best day.

I have talked with many well-educated spiritual leaders who have no sense of how to hear God. Few things sadden my heart more. How do we know what to say or do if we are not listening for and hearing the voice of God?

Once, during a sermon, I asked my congregation how many believed that they had heard God's voice. About one-third of them slowly raised their hands. What I said next was not planned, but very enlightening. I asked, "How many have heard God say 'no'?" Two-thirds of the room quickly raised their hands. Last time I checked, *no* is a word. It's one of the first words we learn as babies.

I have mentored many people who have come to me for direction. One young man had just received a new job offer that would give him more money, better benefits, and the opportunity for more travel. It was amazing. After sharing all the details, he was still struggling with his decision. He had not been at his current position for very long. Was this the right move?

I told him, "Facts are great. They are our friends. But the only real question to ask is: What does God want you to do? The rest is just details."

He didn't know what God wanted him to do, so I asked him if he wanted my help. He replied, "Yes."

Then I said, "I'm going to count down from ten, and when I'm done, I want you to tell me what God wants you to do. Ten. Nine. Eight. Seven. Six."

"Wait, wait, wait," he protested. "I can't do it. It's too hard."

I asked, "You wanted my help, right? Okay then. Five. Four. Three. Two. One."

There was a significant pause, and then he said, "God wants me to stay in my current role."

"Great," I said. "Now, I want you to keep this answer private for one week. Share it with your wife. The two of you pray about it. If it's the wrong decision, God will say 'no,' and you'll know to take the new opportunity. Either way, you have heard from God."

He came by my office the next day to tell me that he and his wife had clarity. They were staying. They were sure that it was what God wanted. They called the people with the new opportunity and told them "no." My friend didn't need to wait a week. He just needed to hear the voice of God.

Why do we always wait until we have a large decision to make before we start to listen for God's voice? It is so much better when we position ourselves to hear God every day.

Jesus said, "I assure you that the time is coming, indeed it's here now, when the dead will hear my voice—the voice of the Son of God. And those who listen will live" (John 5:25). Spiritually dead people come alive when they hear the voice of God. We don't even begin to live the life God has for us until we hear and listen to His voice. As James said, "But don't just listen to God's word. You must do what it says. Otherwise, you are only fooling yourselves" (James 1:22). We read in Hebrews 4:12 that "the word of God is alive and powerful."

It's time to strengthen your partnership with God. Mind the gap between where you are and where God wants you to be. What's your next step? Do you need to position yourself for partnership with Him? Is God asking you to clarify your pre-decisions? Do you need to overcome your fear of change and of being different? Start listening for God's voice daily! It's time for your next step.

THE STORY CONTINUES

As I write this, we just received news that one of the ladies from our recovery program last fall relapsed, overdosed, and died last week. That's hard news to hear, but it is a strong reminder of the critical importance of the lessons we are learning and sharing with others. I don't know why it happened. The complexity of the answer would most likely be way beyond my comprehension.

But this I know: we all need partnership! In our past. In our present. In our future. We were created for partnership. Hopefully your story has included many partners over the years. If so, keep it up. If not, it's time to change your ways. Past partnerships don't replace the need for current and future partnerships. From beginning to end, God has designed us to partner with Him and with others.

What's the good part of partnership? We were made for it. It makes us stronger, more capable, more ready, willing, and able to stand toe to toe with the brokenness of this world. Partnership is transformative. It's a huge part of how Jesus changes us from the inside out.

What's the hard part of partnership? It's hard work! Human brokenness can be daunting. Not to mention God's expectation of vulnerability and faith from us and our lifelong call to listen to Him (and others). Partnership is a great investment. It can be costly, but let's count the cost and engage. It's worth the mess!

Chapter Six Questions

Question: How can you better position yourself to partner with God? Are you pre-decided in your partnership with Him?

_____

_____

_____

_____

_____

_____

_____

_____

_____

Question: How, specifically, does following Jesus shape the way you live your life?

_____

_____

_____

_____

_____

_____

_____

_____

_____

_____

Question: How do you position yourself to hear the voice of God?

_____

_____

_____

_____

_____

_____

_____

_____

_____

_____

_____

_____

Action: Think about areas of your life that don't seem to be affected much by your commitment to following Jesus. Pick one of those areas and offer it to God in prayer. Ask Him to transform it in the way He knows is best.

Identify your first step to giving that part of your life completely to Jesus—and take that step!

Chapter Six Notes

Productivity

REAL STORIES
WILL AND GLORY

Glory was a beautiful, accomplished Tennessee Walker who had to be retired early. She had behavioral problems that led to a serious injury. For some reason, Glory felt the need to protect herself from the other horses, especially when there was food around. She would violently kick the walls of her stall, warning the others to keep away.

No one knew where this behavior came from, but something had to change. Then Glory seriously injured her leg. Her owner, though advised to put her down, decided to give her one more chance. They put chains on her legs while she was in the stall to keep her from kicking. It worked.

Over the years, Glory overcame her fears, and her behavioral issues stopped. She didn't need to wear the chains anymore. Glory was twenty years old when she met Will, a twelve-year-old with issues of his own.

Like Glory, Will had problems with fear and aggression. He came from an abusive background, where he was neglected and starved. He was physically and emotionally abused. He was also isolated. For two years, he was locked in his room. He was finally rescued by extended family, but his journey to wholeness would be rocky.

He had been kept from school during his early developmental years, so he had a lot of catching up to do. It was hard for him to trust anyone. He kept quiet and didn't speak unless he absolutely had to. He did not like to be touched at all. He would steal food and hide it in his room to keep it from being eaten by others.

Like Glory, he did not want to socialize with others and would fight to keep his space secure. His isolation kept him from developing the socialization skills necessary for successful growth into adolescence. Then, one summer, the principal of his alternative school sent some of her students to horse camp. Will was selected and partnered with Glory. Sounds like something God would arrange.

Glory was patient and calm with Will. She waited and waited for him to make first contact. She greeted him with a good attitude and showed him her willingness to trust him as she followed his lead. Will felt safe with her. By the end of the first day, he was asking to go back to her stall to say goodbye.

Will was not one to be touched. He would wince at the slightest brush on the shoulder and did not like to touch others. But with Glory, he loved to rub her, brush her, and talk to her. He also loved to be touched by her. When she turned to see what he was doing, he felt like someone noticed him. Back at school, his counselors noticed the change. They were seeing big improvements in his behavior.

Glory and Will quickly became good friends. Sometimes he would lean against Glory for support, and she would rub against him to satisfy that little itch on her neck. Will felt understood for the first time. Glory felt his true sense of sadness. Each session, she stood there, patiently waiting for him to feel comfortable with her. She did not walk away or ignore him. She stood by him. She understood his hesitations because she had lived with similar fears herself.

Through the investment of love, patience, and partnership with humans, Glory learned to overcome her fears. Glory was now making a similar investment in Will. She saw him for who he really was and his need to learn to trust and communicate. She was willing to help him slow down enough to take a deeper look inside himself.

To What End?

We believe in the power of heart change, but to what end? We have discussed the layers of heart work necessary to position ourselves for partnership with God. But wait, there's more. God wants your heart change to cause you to flourish. He wants the productivity of your life to be multiplied "thirty, sixty, and even a hundred times" (Matthew 13:8).

Following Jesus adds so much to our lives. He said, "Come to me, all of you who are weary and carry heavy burdens, and I will give you rest. Take my yoke upon you. Let me teach you, because I am humble and gentle at heart, and you will find rest for your souls. For my yoke is easy to bear, and the burden I give you is light" (Matthew 11:28–30).

This easy, light, and restful life is not meant to be a life lived in neutral. Quite the opposite. Following Jesus leads to a full and productive life. Jesus said, "Yes, I am the vine; you are the branches. Those who remain in me, and I in them, will produce much fruit. For apart from me you can do nothing" (John 15:5).

Jesus "gave his life to free us from every kind of sin, to cleanse us, and to make us his very own people, totally committed to doing good deeds" (Titus 2:14). Paul wrote, "Our people must learn to do good by meeting the urgent needs of others; then they will not be unproductive" (Titus 3:14). Paul also said, "Never get tired of doing good" (2 Thessalonians 3:13).

Yes, Jesus wants us to live productive lives, but many Christ-followers get confused at this point. Many think that being a Christ-follower is all about doing things *for* Jesus. That's not the productivity He is looking for. Jesus told us that on judgment day, many people will try to list all the things they have done for Him. They're missing the point. He is more interested in what they have done *with* Him and *in* Him. He will tell those who try to impress Him with their own efforts, "I never knew you. Get away from me" (Matthew 7:22–23). The productivity Jesus seeks happens in relationship. Partnership matters if we are to be productive followers of Jesus.

OWN YOUR STUFF

Describe a person who takes responsibility for his or her own life, partners with God, sets boundaries, leaves margin, and chooses to live as a wise person. What is that person like? What is the end result of his or her life?

Now describe a person who doesn't own his or her stuff, who doesn't take responsibility for the human part of the partnership. What is that person like? What is his or her life like? This is all too predictable.

Whom do you want to become?

Jesus told a story about a businessman who had three people working for him (Matthew 25:14–30). He had to leave town. Before he left, he invested in each of them according to the person's proven productivity. He wanted his business to grow while he was gone. One received five bags of silver, another two, and the last one only one bag of silver. Their work would be measured based on what each could handle. When the businessman was ready to leave, he said, "Make me proud."

When the boss returned, the first two guys had doubled their boss's money. He said to each of them, "Well done, my good and faithful servant. You have been faithful in handling this small amount, so now I will give you many more responsibilities. Let's celebrate together!" (Matthew 25:21, 23). Hopefully by now, you've noticed that Jesus loves a story that ends with a good party!

How many of us want to hear those same words at the end of our lives? Those words will be the single most important thing in that moment. It won't matter how easy or hard, how long or short your life has been. It won't matter if you were rich or poor, healthy or sick, good-looking or looking good. All that will matter will be the words of Jesus: "Well done, my good and faithful servant" (Matthew 25:21, 23).

The third guy, afraid that he might mess up, buried everything his boss gave him and had nothing to show for his life. He thought that he was playing it safe. It turns out that he was wasting what he was given.

The problem with this story is that most of us, if we're being honest, relate most closely with this third guy. We don't see ourselves as having been given a lot of opportunity and wealth to work with. Not even an average amount. We see ourselves as the one who was given only a little from God. We are tempted to play it safe. As a result, we lack productivity, and God is not happy with us.

When I say to "own your stuff," I mean all of it: your thoughts, your feelings, your choices, your actions, your accomplishments, your failures, your consequences, your attitudes, and your productivity. Own all that is yours to do and be. God has invested in you, and He is expecting you to do something with it.

The first two guys in this story did exceptionally well with their responsibilities, and their boss threw them a party. What about those of us who do just a little with what we have been given? Will we get a participation trophy, a plaque, or special recognition? I don't think so.

Jesus actually asked the same question: "And does the master thank the servant for doing what he was told to do?

Of course not. In the same way, when you obey me you should say, 'We are unworthy servants who have simply done our duty'" (Luke 17:9–10). Given our current culture, those are hard words to hear, but they are true nonetheless. We are honored when God chooses to use us for His purposes. Our reward is to hear, "Well done."

How will your story end? God wants to throw a party to celebrate what you have done with your life. What's the catch? You have to do something. You have to be productive. You have to embrace your calling and responsibility from God and follow through with what He gives you to do. To be clear, the productivity that matters is the fruit of God's leading and direction in your life, not random, self-directed busyness. It will take a personal, intimate relationship with God to know what to do.

SET BOUNDARIES

Have you ever noticed Jesus' boundaries? There are times when we have difficulty understanding Jesus' behavior (on the outside) because we don't understand His boundaries (on the inside). He got angry and chased people out of the temple with a homemade whip (John 2:15). He didn't take time to interact with His family when they came to visit with Him (Matthew 12:47–50). He said, "Get away from me, Satan!" to one of His closest friends (Matthew 16:23). What was going on? Boundaries. Those people were out of bounds and wanted Jesus to follow their lead. His road comes with boundaries.

117

Is Jesus' narrow road primarily about external behavior or internal heart change? The boundaries for His narrow, difficult road are, first and foremost, internal. When we follow Him, we will live from the heart. Our perceptions and motivations must be shaped and directed by Him. We will hear His voice on the inside, and as we do, we will become more and more like Him on the outside. As we walk with Him, Jesus will clarify for us those things that are ours to do, and we will do them. We won't define our boundaries; Jesus will.

There have always been those who love the notion of living life on a broad road with no boundaries. They call it freedom. Their freedom is nothing like the freedom Jesus offers. It is based on living out their personal truth. They pursue personal sovereignty, staying in control of their little kingdom.

Following Jesus means that we find freedom in walking on a pre-decided, narrow, difficult road. His road. Are you interested?

Jesus taught, "If any of you wants to be my follower, you must give up your own way, take up your cross daily, and follow me. If you try to hang on to your life, you will lose it. But if you give up your life for my sake, you will save it. And what do you benefit if you gain the whole world but are yourself lost or destroyed?" (Luke 9:23–25).

In the verse just before this, He gave us a quick peek at the things that were His to do. He said, "The Son of Man must suffer many terrible things. ... He will be rejected by the elders, the leading priests, and the teachers of religious law.

He will be killed, but on the third day he will be raised from the dead" (Luke 9:22).

Jesus didn't delegate His cross to His twelve disciples. He didn't say, "Hey, Peter, I could really use your help. I need you to suffer many terrible things for Me. If you could take that off My plate, that would be great. James, if you could be rejected by the elders. John, if you could take on the priests and the teachers of religious law. And finally, Andrew, if you could be killed for Me and, on the third day, rise from the dead, that would make My life so much easier." No. He embraced His cross for us.

In the same way, we must own the boundaries of our calling. Now it's our turn to embrace our difficulties for Him. Like Jesus, we don't get to pass off our responsibilities to others, nor do we pick up other people's responsibilities for them. Our crosses may include some of the very sufferings asked of Christ, but He shouldered His cross, and now we must shoulder ours.

Don't get me wrong. We are absolutely supposed to help people with their burdens. But there's a difference between a load and a burden. We all have our own loads to carry, our personal responsibilities, our own crosses to bear. But sometimes a person's load becomes an overload, a burden, and it's too much for him or her to handle alone.

How do we know when to help and when to let someone carry his or her own load? Paul clarified this balancing act for us: "Share each other's burdens [overload], and in this way obey the law of Christ. If you think you are too important to help someone, you are only fooling yourself. You are not that important. Pay careful attention to your own work [load], for then you will get the satisfaction of a job well done, and you won't need to compare yourself to anyone else. For we are each responsible for our own conduct [load]" (Galatians 6:2–5).

Yes, we are all responsible for our own stuff, but sometimes our load becomes an overload. Sometimes we need help. At other times, we need to help others, not with their load—because we're not supposed to do their work for them—but with their overload.

LEAVE MARGIN

Jesus owned His stuff and knew His boundaries, which enabled Him to have time for the unplanned interruptions of life. He also never filled His life to overflowing to prove His productivity to God or to others. Jesus left room for the messiness of life to happen. I'm guessing that He planned for the unplanned. He expected the unexpected. He might even have looked forward to it.

When someone asks how we're doing, the socially acceptable response is: "Busy." It doesn't even matter why we're busy. We think that if we're busy, it must be good. If we're not busy, we must not be that important.

Life needs margin. Relationships need margin. Marriage needs margin. Parenting needs margin. Your work needs margin. Your budget needs margin. Your vacation needs margin. Your FOMO (fear of missing out) needs margin. Yet, we are often draining the margin out of our lives. The lesson to be learned: order your life to build margin over time.

When COVID-19 first hit, many people from my church said to me, "I have a fully funded emergency fund, and I've hardly had to use it. This COVID situation might become an emergency for some. If you learn of anyone who needs help, let me know." Throughout the COVID pandemic, our church had more than enough margin to meet all of the needs.

LIVE LIKE THOSE WHO ARE WISE

Wisdom comes from perspective. When we walk in wisdom, it's because we have gained perspective from life experience, other people, and, most importantly, God. Jesus lived from God's perspective. If we want to be wise, so should we: "If you are wise and understand God's ways, prove it by living an honorable life, doing good works with the humility that comes from wisdom" (James 3:13).

In order to make the most of our lives, Paul advised us, "So be careful how you live. Don't live like fools, but like those who are wise" (Ephesians 5:15). Did you notice that he didn't say to *be* wise? He said to *live like* (or as) those who are wise. That feels more doable. Doesn't it? It should.

Solomon, the man who was reported to be the wisest man who ever lived, finished his life living *like* a fool, so the end of his life did not turn out well for him. Even though he had been exceptionally wise most of his life, he crashed and burned in the end.

I'm sure that the thief hanging on the cross next to Jesus

had done a lot of foolish things that led him to being executed on a cross. Most likely, none of his friends or family would have described him as wise. Yet, in the end, he decided to do something a wise person would do. He chose to respect God and put his faith in Christ. Jesus said to him, "I assure you, today you will be with me in paradise" (Luke 23:43). That's a good ending. Not because he lived a wise life, but because when the moment came to make his decision about Jesus, he chose to do what a wise person would do.

THE STORY CONTINUES

Will's partnership with Glory made a big difference for Will. There was a noticeable change taking place in that season of his life. But was that the end of his story or just the beginning? His relationship with Glory set him up for a better, more productive life in the future. The changes would be more than momentary.

As horse camp ended, Will's counselors noticed significant changes in him. He was voluntarily speaking out more in class and had a smile on his face that was rarely seen before. He had something to say and was no longer afraid to let others know it. He didn't cringe when someone touched him gently on the shoulder. Will's heart change at camp was translating into a better, brighter future. His healing process had begun.

Chapter Seven Questions

Question: Describe a person who takes responsibility for his or her own life, partners with God, sets boundaries, leaves margin, and chooses to live like a wise person. What is that person like? What is his or her life like?

_____

_____

_____

_____

_____

_____

_____

_____

_____

Question: Now describe a person who doesn't own his or her stuff, the human part of the partnership. What is that person like? What is his or her life like?

_____

_____

_____

_____

_____

_____

_____

_____

_____

_____

Question: How well are you embracing your difficulties for Jesus? What responsibilities are you carrying? In what areas of your life are you relying on others to carry responsibilities that are yours? In what ways are you trying to shoulder others' responsibilities?

_____

_____

_____

_____

_____

_____

_____

_____

_____

_____

_____

_____

Action: What is draining the margin out of your life? List the following areas of life and any others you can think of:

- work / school

- budget / money

- marriage / romantic relationship

- family / parenting

For each area you listed, consider how much margin you have. What do you feel is draining your margin in each area?

Reflect and pray about specific ways you can create more margin in your life to make you more productive *in partnership with God*. Write down three of those ways and come up with a plan for putting each of those margin-building changes into effect over the next month—beginning this week!

Chapter Seven Notes

_____

_____

_____

_____

_____

_____

_____

_____

_____

_____

_____

_____

_____

_____

_____

_____

_____

CHAPTER EIGHT

Embrace the Mess

REAL STORIES
JESSICA AND KAI

I (Jessica) have struggled to treat my addiction for four years. My life's been a complete mess. I have found no relief or hope. Through my addiction recovery program and equine therapy, I am learning to live beyond the destruction, despair, mess, and trauma that have clouded my life for so long.

I am learning to look to God's Word for truth about myself. While I do learn and grow from reading God's Word, I have learned so much more by experiencing it played out through equine therapy. It has taught me to embrace the messiness of my life. It has brought me a deeper understanding and freedom from the bondage I lay in for so long.

I see the change in others, and I want it, too. I see a light in their eyes, a gentleness in their touch, and enough vulnerability to believe that it's possible for me as well. The horses and the people working with them have shown me patience, wisdom, faith, and transparency. I see Christ at work, and I am grateful.

My life was a mess in general, and Kai helped me to see some of the specifics. When I asked him to do different tasks, he would get bracey, self-protective, uncooperative, and resistant. Working with an untrusting, obstinate horse was frustrating me. Then my instructor explained Kai's behavior to me, and I realized that he was just mirroring me. I had to change my own behavior, my own strategy, if I was going to win Kai's trust.

Kai helped me to see that I was bracey in my relationships with God and with others. I was closed off, and that didn't work. I didn't want to give up control any more than Kai did. Kai didn't want me to be the boss of him or even a partner because he didn't trust me. I had to settle down and give him good reason to see me as trustworthy. I also needed to settle down and see how many times God had shown Himself trustworthy in my life.

Kai taught me that it's possible to work through the mess, and now I am walking in a new direction. The mess doesn't have to define me. Vulnerability is key. It doesn't mean demise. God has shown me that I can be vulnerable not only with Him, but also with others.

I learned to have a relationship of trust without a need for manipulation. I don't have to control people. If I want to be loved and find intimacy, I must open my heart and life. With

God, I won't be left behind, and I will find healing. I thank God for the horses and humans who have spoken into my life. Following Jesus is messy because life is messy, but following Jesus makes life worth the mess.

WE WERE MADE TO EMBRACE THE MESS

Think about it: in the beginning, what was humanity's job? What did God create us for? God designed humanity to partner with Him in subduing, developing, and caring for the earth. God planned for Adam and Eve eventually to venture out from the garden, embrace the chaos of an untamed world, and be part of creating a beautiful one. He designed us to care for all His creatures and their environment. Sounds like humanity was made to get our hands dirty.

God created Adam and Eve to "fill the earth and govern it" (Genesis 1:28). They were not called to stay in the garden. They were called to subdue a feral world. After they sinned, things got messier. But God still expected them to be an influence for good and to do what was right, with creation and with each other. God warned their son Cain to do the right thing or sin would control his life (Genesis 4:7). Sin is controlling, and it makes human existence much messier.

Cain was to care for his younger brother, Abel, but instead he attacked him and killed him. When God asked Cain what happened to Abel, Cain responded with the age-old question: "Am I my brother's guardian?" (Genesis 4:9). If you've never taken time to figure it out, the answer was and still is "yes." We were made to care for creation and each other.

Fast forward to Jesus' birth. He came to embrace the mess. He could have influenced, healed, and transformed us from a distance, but He didn't. He did not turn away from our challenging, chaotic lives. Jesus chose to step into our world and embrace us in our mess. It was His calling. As a result, His experience on earth was messy from beginning to end.

Humanity was created with a stunning capacity to embrace the mess. We were designed by God to make a difference by living sacrificially for God and others. Jesus said that we would be His "salt" and "light" in the world (Matthew 5:13–16). Both metaphors point to influence. Salt has an invisible influence, and light has a visible influence. Both influences are unavoidable. We were designed to have an influence in this world, for good or for evil. Jesus calls us to use our visible and invisible influence for Him.

Jesus had a term for people who are called to embrace the mess in life intentionally. He called them *shepherds*. He saw Himself as the "good shepherd" (John 10:11), which means that He lived sacrificially for the good of others. In the culture of His day, being a shepherd was not a badge of honor. It was the ultimate dirty job. Sheep unavoidably rub off on those who are helping them. Shepherds were considered second-class citizens, in part because hanging out with a flock of sheep 24/7 is a dirty, stinky job. Sheep are messy.

CALLED BY GOD

We have the capacity to embrace the mess of our world. The responsibility of shepherding was given to Adam and Eve, Abel, Noah, Abraham, Isaac, Jacob (Israel), Joseph, Moses, and David. All these heroes of the faith were literal shepherds who became spiritual shepherds of God's people as they partnered with God, the ultimate Shepherd.

David related to God as his Shepherd: "The LORD is my shepherd; I have all that I need" (Psalm 23:1). Similarly, he said, "We are his people, the sheep of his pasture" (Psalm 100:3). But God also said to David, "You will be the shepherd of my people Israel. You will be Israel's leader" (2 Samuel 5:2). God was declaring that His leaders and influencers would shepherd His people with Him: "He chose his servant David, calling him from the sheep pens. He took David from tending the ewes and lambs and made him the shepherd of Jacob's descendants—God's own people, Israel" (Psalm 78:70–71).

When the nation of Israel lost sight of this calling and stopped taking spiritual responsibility for each other, they lost the blessing of God: "The shepherds of my people have lost their senses. They no longer seek wisdom from the LORD. Therefore, they fail completely, and their flocks are scattered" (Jeremiah 10:21). Likewise, God said, "My people have been lost sheep. Their shepherds have led them astray and turned them loose in the mountains. They have lost their way and can't remember how to get back to the sheepfold" (Jeremiah 50:6).

Before we look down on these ancient believers, let's take stock of how we are doing. Have we embraced our call to care for others in Jesus' name? Has the church in America kept or lost its bearings? Do we see ourselves as shepherds who are strong for the weak or as something less?

Throughout the pages of the Old Testament, God promised a coming Messiah, a Shepherd of His people (Ezekiel 34:23; 37:24–28) who would "stand to lead his flock with the LORD's strength" (Micah 5:4). When Jesus was born and Herod was frantic to find and destroy the child, his scholars pointed him to Bethlehem to find "the shepherd for my people Israel" (Matthew 2:6).

WHAT IF JESUS WASN'T
TALKING ONLY TO PETER?

Jesus had many conversations with His disciples after His resurrection (Acts 1:3). Final words are often the most significant. With the words of His final conversations, Jesus was preparing His disciples for their calling. He was equipping them to launch the Church.

Jesus instructed His disciples to wait until they received the Holy Spirit. Those first disciples positioned themselves in obedience to be empowered by God. As a result, they were part of the initial outpouring of the Holy Spirit. And God has continued to pour out His Spirit on all who position themselves for His service.

Many Christ-followers believe that when Jesus said, "Go

into all the world and preach the Good News to everyone" (Mark 16:15) and "make disciples of all the nations" (Matthew 28:18–20), He wasn't just talking to the eleven remaining disciples, but to all of us. They believe that it's the responsibility of all Jesus' followers, the whole church, to make disciples. In short, disciples are to make disciples who make disciples. I would agree.

Three times Jesus asked Peter, "Do you love Me?" Three times Peter answered, "Yes" (John 21:15–19). Each time, Jesus responded with the call to feed and care for His sheep. I don't believe that Jesus was talking only to Peter. Shepherding is the shared spiritual responsibility of all maturing believers who love Jesus. Shepherds are to make shepherds who make shepherds. This would raise the bar on what it means to follow Jesus. It would change the way we see ourselves. It would inform our mission, our role, our responsibility, and our authority.

"I DON'T THINK I'M CUT OUT FOR THIS"

Who in the Bible was best suited to be a shepherd of God's people? Whom would you pick—maybe Peter, Barnabas, Moses, or Paul?

It must be Peter. He was personally handpicked by Jesus to shepherd the early church, perhaps because he was an influencer, a leader, and an initiator. No one was more persuasive than Peter. But sadly, he was also impulsive, disorganized, undisciplined, and easily angered. He lacked follow-through. Hmm.

You might lean toward Barnabas over Peter. His name meant "son of encouragement" (Acts 4:36), and encouragement might just be the number one requirement for being a shepherd. Barnabas was also a peacemaker. He was loyal, caring, steady, patient, full of grace, and amazingly good under pressure. He was clearly the best fit for the job—until you consider that he was also a reluctant leader. He was indecisive and overly cautious, and he balked at making hard decisions. As a result, he and Paul had to part ways over working with John Mark.

Let's look at Moses, our Old Testament hero. He did a commendable job of shepherding Israel through forty years in the wilderness (Exodus 12–40). Before that, he had spent many years shepherding actual sheep. That must have been helpful. Besides, Moses was really big on doing things right. He was conscientious, deliberate, and exceptionally self-disciplined. He was a ponderer and a finisher. He's got to be our man—except for the fact that he was also an unconfident leader, negative, critical, rigid, hard to please, and easily hurt.

Which leaves us Paul. Good choice. Paul was a doer. He got things done. He was unstoppable, strong, goal-oriented, determined, and decisive. But he wasn't very warm and fuzzy. Aren't spiritual shepherds supposed to be warm and fuzzy? Paul could be impatient, harsh, sarcastic, domineering, insensitive, and opinionated. So, I guess it's none of the above.

Actually, it was all of the above. They were four of the most significant shepherds in the history of God's people, yet God gave them different gifts, strengths, and weaknesses.

Each one leveraged his strengths for the good of God's people. They partnered with other shepherds to overcome their weaknesses. They were not meant to shepherd alone, and neither are we.

Which one or two of these shepherds are you most like? Given your own strengths and weaknesses, which do you resemble? More importantly, how will you leverage your personal God-given strengths for the good of God's people?

Accept Authority and Responsibility

Shepherds embrace their authority and responsibility. Paul explained, "Our authority builds you up; it doesn't tear you down. So I will not be ashamed of using my authority" (2 Corinthians 10:8). Our culture balks at authority. Many believers today hold back from ministry because they don't want to take on any authority or responsibility. Shepherds are people who step up.

A Roman centurion—an oppressor of Israel, a high-ranking "bad guy"—came to Jesus because he was desperate. His servant was paralyzed and in misery. He wanted Jesus to heal his servant, but he said, "Lord, I am not worthy to have you come into my home. Just say the word from where you are, and my servant will be healed" (Matthew 8:8). The centurion understood the power of authority, which impressed Jesus: "When Jesus heard this, he was amazed. Turning to those who were following him, he said, 'I tell you the truth, I haven't seen faith like this in all Israel!'" (Matthew 8:10).

Before ascending to heaven, Jesus said, "I have been given all authority in heaven and on earth. Therefore, go and make disciples of all the nations" (Matthew 28:18–19). Jesus walked in His authority as our Shepherd, and now we need to do the same. We have been given authority and responsibility to build people up!

The Holy Spirit, like Jesus, encourages us. In fact, Jesus referred to the Holy Spirit as our "Advocate" (John 14:16) or "Helper" (ESV). We are called to do and be like Him—to help, comfort, encourage, exhort, and speak into people's lives. To come alongside and help. To build others up in Jesus' name. That is the nature of our authority.

Embrace the Prodigal

It's important to recognize that accepting our authority and responsibility will lead us to difficult, inconvenient, and uncomfortable places. Are we willing to accept the messiness of our call?

The acknowledged shepherds of Jesus' day—Pharisees, Sadducees, and teachers of the Law—didn't think that getting messy was part of their job description: "Tax collectors and other notorious sinners [really messy people] often came to listen to Jesus teach. This made the Pharisees and teachers of religious law complain that he was associating with such sinful [messy and undesirable] people—even eating with them!" (Luke 15:1–2). They would never have allowed themselves to be caught embracing the mess.

So, Jesus told them a series of parables, including the story of the prodigal son (which we considered in Chapter Four). Where do you see yourself in that parable? Some identify with the younger brother, some with the older brother. Many say that they want to be the father. Technically, that part is taken. The father in the story represents God. But we are all supposed to grow up to be like our Father (Ephesians 5:1). If that's true, we all become people who love and embrace the prodigals in our lives.

When should we embrace the prodigals? When do we expose ourselves to their messy, stinky lives? The "when" is important. There are three indicators that the moment is right. First, we embrace them when God breaks through their hard, cluttered hearts and they see their need for Him. Second, we embrace them when they start taking steps toward home. It's impossible to embrace someone who is walking the other way. Finally, we don't wait until they are all the way home. We run to embrace them on their journey home, even when they are "still a long way off" (Luke 15:20).

Be a Friend of Sinners

When Matthew chose to follow Jesus, Jesus went to Matthew's celebration party and befriended his friends (Matthew 9:10). When Zacchaeus came down out of the tree, Jesus invited Himself over to Zacchaeus's house and befriended him (Luke 19:1–10).

Was Zacchaeus a "prodigal"? He was moving toward Jesus. He was coming to his senses. He was still a long way off. Yes, yes, and yes! So, it was time for Jesus to embrace the prodigal and make a friend.

What happened next? People grumbled. Closed-hearted people often grumble, but Jesus didn't. And Zacchaeus's heart flew wide open. He believed, and his life was transformed! Jesus had found another lost sheep of Israel.

Be Unoffendable

Jesus also showed us that good shepherds are not easily offended. How did He relate to run-of-the-mill sinners? He wasn't quick to be offended by the messiness of their lives. He wasn't focused on their sins, but rather on the condition and direction of their hearts.

Why is being unoffendable so important for a shepherd? Solomon said, "An offended friend is harder to win back than a fortified city" (Proverbs 18:19). Hearts that are offended slam shut in self-protection mode. Jesus doesn't want that for us. He instructed us to be intentional with people who sin against us. He wants us to "go privately and point out the offense" (Matthew 18:15). Why? Because He doesn't want other people's sin to become an offense to us. He doesn't want us to harden our hearts.

The woman caught in the act of adultery offended the religious leaders. They became very demanding. They insisted that something must be done (John 8:1–11). Offended people are often very demanding. What if Jesus had been easily offended by her sins? That's not Jesus.

Jesus asked a question to challenge and enlighten the hearts of the religious leaders. He wanted to help them see what they weren't seeing. He said, "All right, but let the one who has never sinned throw the first stone!" (John 8:7). One by one, they dropped their stones and walked away. Once they were all gone, Jesus built the woman up, giving her unexpected grace and truth and pointing her in a new direction, the right direction.

Being offended is not a sign of personal purity but of pride. Pride makes messy lives messier. Our reaction to messy people reveals to us the true condition of our own hearts.

Do What's Best for Others

What about the money changers in the temple? Wasn't He offended by them? What was motivating Jesus when He made a whip out of rope to drive them from the temple (John 2:13–16)? Clearly, the issue was their offensive behavior toward the temple of God, but there was more to it.

Jesus always did what was best for people. The love of God leaves no other option. We know that "God opposes the proud but gives grace to the humble" (James 4:6; 1 Peter 5:5). But why? It's *not* because He loves humble people and hates proud people. He loves them all. Jesus' public opposition to the money changers' proud, out-of-bounds behavior was the best thing for them. They needed to recognize the seriousness of their sin.

With God, opposition isn't the same as judgment. It isn't personal rejection. God opposes the proud because that's what they need to wake up and smell the coffee. Proud people are on the wide road to self-destruction. God opposes them because He wants them to humble themselves and be saved. So should we. If someone you love were standing on a train track, with a train closing in, would you not assert yourself, risk your life, push him or her out of the way, and save your loved one's life? That's what shepherds do.

Treat the Humble with Respect

Shepherds do what's best for others, oppose the proud, and give grace to the humble. Admittedly, in our culture, this is getting more and more difficult. I mourn the loss of humility. People, young and old, rich and poor, are taught to throw off humility and embrace pride. The loss of humility is condemning our culture. God blesses those with humble hearts.

There was a time when Jesus "had to go through Samaria" on His way from Jerusalem to Galilee (John 4:3–4). That makes no sense. Jews of His day would do almost anything to avoid taking that route. He had to go through Samaria because there was a woman there who had been humbled by her incredibly messy life. She was a Samaritan. (Strike one.) She was a woman, a second-class citizen in those days. (Strike two.) She had been married five times and was now living with a guy she wasn't married to. (Strike three!) Her life was an absolute mess.

Jesus' unexpected and unpredictable grace shocked this woman, the villagers, and His disciples. What was He up to? He was seeking and saving the lost. He was treating a humbled woman with respect. He was focused on her heart, not her sin. He was looking to build her up, not tear her down. He was being the good Shepherd.

As you prepare to follow the good Shepherd, ask yourself these questions:

- How's your heart?

- Are you ready, willing, and able to partner with God and other maturing believers in shepherding God's flock?

- Are you willing to pick up your God-given authority and responsibility?

- Are you willing to encourage others and build them up?

- Are you willing to embrace the prodigal, be a friend of sinners, be unoffendable, and treat the humble with respect?

This is God's call when we choose to love and follow Jesus.

THE STORY CONTINUES

Jessica completed her addiction recovery program a truly changed person. She had extended her time in the program by three months to make sure that would be true. She had come into the program under protest but left with a new faith and renewed confidence. She re-entered her career as an ER nurse and proceeded to live her happily-ever-after.

Well, that's how we all want the story to end, right? It's what Jessica wanted. It's why she had worked so long and so hard. She, too, thought that she was well on her way to her personal happily-ever-after.

That's the problem, isn't it? Wrong thinking. The truth is that the story never ends; it just continues. We don't get to "arrive." We don't get to let down our guard. We don't get to settle down in our own personal "promised land" and return to our self-sufficient ways. Surprisingly, the stronger Diane became in herself, the more her need and desire for God began to wane.

In time, she drifted from God and relapsed. For a season, she was able to keep it hidden from her friends. Finally, she came to herself and said, "Even if I have to go back to square one, even if I embarrass myself, even if I lose my friendships, even if I lose my career, I will stick with this journey. I will return to God. I will be changed and ever-changing!"

Jessica is back, working with Kai and embracing her next season of transformation. She is inspiring others and making a difference.

Chapter Eight Questions

Question: Given your own strengths and weaknesses, which do you think you most resemble: Moses, Peter, Barnabas, or Paul?

_____

_____

_____

_____

_____

_____

_____

_____

_____

_____

Question: How can you leverage your personal God-given strengths for the good of God's people?

_____

_____

_____

_____

_____

_____

_____

_____

_____

_____

Question: How would you define or describe your God-given authority and responsibility?

_____

_____

_____

_____

_____

Action: Rate your relative strength from (1) strongest to (7) weakest in the aspects of following Jesus listed below:

- Accept authority and responsibility.

- Encourage others and build them up.

- Be a friend of sinners.

- Be unoffendable.

- Do what's best for others.

- Treat the humble with respect.

In which of these attitudes and habits are you strongest? Where do you have the most room to grow?

Circle the aspect of following Jesus that you numbered (7). Now find and write down two verses from the New Testament to help remind and encourage you to let God work in that area.

Chapter Eight Notes

_____

_____

_____

_____

_____

_____

_____

_____

_____

_____

_____

_____

_____

_____

_____

_____

Settle Down, Settle Down

REAL STORIES
DI AND T-BEAR

This is my (Di's) second time working through the Hearts in Harmony program with T-Bear. He's an amazing horse. Not so much the first time we worked together, but this time was different. Because I was different. It was T-Bear who showed me the difference. I didn't realize that he would be more than my partner in this program. He would become my teacher.

When I first met T-Bear, I was wound pretty tight. Stubborn. Willful. I thought that these horse exercises would be about me getting the horse to do things my way. I still had many walls up in my life, and I didn't want them torn down. I didn't want anyone to see or know my weaknesses.

In the first go-around, I was stressed, so T-Bear was stressed. I was insecure and unsure about who I was and what

I was doing. I thought I wasn't letting it show. I wanted and needed to maintain control. I would not be surrendering to anyone, especially not a horse. But by the end, I was slowly seeing some things I hadn't noticed before. The first time around was a good first step.

This second time with T-Bear was noticeably different. He was not as unconfident as I had originally thought he was. In fact, he had been mirroring my lack of confidence in myself back to me. He was picking up on my fear, anger, and anxiety, but as I settled down, so did he. My need to be in control was dissipating.

This time T-Bear allowed me to lead him. He was more open because I was more open, very much like the way I was opening to God and letting Him lead my life. T-Bear was no longer stubborn or tense. He was trusting me. His trust was a direct reflection of my growing trust and relationship with God and others.

SETTLE YOURSELF

Horses know instinctively that they are born into an unsafe world full of predators. They start out suspicious of anything new or different. They see almost everything, including people, as unsafe until proven otherwise. To settle a horse, we must earn its trust, which requires us to settle ourselves first and lead by example.

How many of us who experienced the first year of the COVID pandemic felt unsafe, out of control, stressed, worried, anxious, or angry during that time? National and world events like the pandemic stress us out as a culture.

What we're talking about in this chapter is not a small side issue. Learning to settle ourselves and live in the peace of God is a challenge we all face on a regular basis. In this culture of busyness, we are prone to walking around continually stressed out. It's not good. Jesus has so much more for us. Our unsafe world repeatedly triggers stress in our lives. It's what we do with those feelings of stress, fear, anxiety, and anger that matters. These internal responses to our stress can be suppressed for a season, but in the end, they will come out.

The question is: Will we let these stressors take control of our lives and decision-making? It's not okay to let our hearts be choked out by the cares, riches, and pleasures of life. We must learn to guard our hearts.

Part of the dark side of worry, anger, fear, and anxiety is that they keep us from stepping up and being the people God wants us to be. For instance, some of us get excited about the notion that God wants us to partner with Him and embrace the mess of being His shepherds in the world. Others find that idea overwhelming. It stresses them out. It keeps them from embracing their God-given authority and responsibility as His children.

Shepherding others has the potential to raise our stress level. We will need to be strong. We must manage our stress so we will have the margin we need to be God's salt and light in the world.

Horses help all kinds of humans in all kinds of ways. A common denominator in their helpfulness is their ability to help humans overcome their stress. The stress of disruption or change. The stress of reversal. Stress at work. Stress at home. Stress with finances. The stress of a worldwide pandemic. The stress of rising social tensions. The stress of past abuse, neglect, or PTSD. The stress of a wounded heart. The stress that leads to feelings of tension, depression, frustration, fear, worry, anxiety, anger, and even hatred.

Don't let these negative forces go unchecked. Don't deny them if they are present, but don't let them rule or ruin your life, either. Working with horses can help us to identify and conquer these negative realities.

Jesus said, "I am leaving you with a gift—peace of mind and heart. And the peace I give is a gift the world cannot give. So don't be troubled or afraid" (John 14:27). When fear, worry, anxiety, and anger come knocking on your door, don't make up the guest bedroom. In our broken world, they will want to come and stay for an extended visit. When they show up on your doorstep, remember that the guest room is already spoken for. The peace of Christ has moved in.

Settle Your Fear

Four of the core disciples were experienced fishermen, but one day as they were traveling by boat, a storm blew up, and even the fishermen were terrified. In a panic, they woke Jesus from His nap. Jesus responded to their fears: "When Jesus woke up, he rebuked the wind and said to the waves, 'Silence! Be still!' Suddenly the wind stopped, and there was a great calm" (Mark 4:39). This real act in real time illustrated what Christ does for His followers daily on a heart level. He speaks to the chaos and stress in their lives, and suddenly there is a great calm.

Then Jesus asked the disciples, "Why are you afraid? Do you still have no faith?" (Mark 4:40). From Jesus' perspective, they didn't have a fear problem. Their problem was a lack of faith. They were not leaning into the great calm that comes from being with Jesus. They needed real, tangible faith. They needed the peace of Christ. And so do we.

On another occasion, Jesus sent His disciples ahead by boat while He stayed back to pray. To catch up with them, Jesus decided to walk across the lake on the water. When the disciples saw Him, they freaked out. Jesus said, "Don't be afraid.... Take courage. I am here!" (Matthew 14:27). Why did they freak out? Because, just like with horses, new and unusual experiences often create fear in us.

Jesus expected His disciples to take courage because He was there. They were with Him. We all need the presence of Christ in our hearts and lives if we are going to "settle down, settle down," in the face of our fears. When we are afraid, we need more peace, more faith in God, and more Spirit-empowered courage found in the presence of Christ.

Paul added, "For God has not given us a spirit of fear and timidity, but of power, love, and self-discipline" (2 Timothy 1:7). How are followers of Christ to overcome our fear-based, negative internal narratives? We need to trust the God-given peace, faith, courage, power, love, and self-discipline. It all works. It's all helpful. The presence of God in our lives changes our internal and external realities.

Settle Your Worry

Worry is part of our internal reality. It's a negative interpretation of the unknown and the yet-to-be-determined. In other words, it's another stress-related corruptor of our internal narrative, the story we tell ourselves about ourselves and our lives.

We all know that the world is not perfect. Bad things happen. People who are prone to worry are quick to believe that the worst-case scenario is coming their way. When they worry, it messes with their heads, hearts, and physical well-being. They embrace a negative possibility as truth.

Jesus said to His disciples, "So don't worry about tomorrow, for tomorrow will bring its own worries. Today's trouble is enough for today" (Matthew 6:34). When we worry, we ruin the present with something in the future that may not even happen.

Peter exhorts you to "give all your worries and cares to God, for he cares about you" (1 Peter 5:7). Peter was saying to give God your anxiety, including all the thoughts and feelings that want to tear you apart from the inside out. Why? Because God is watching over you. He is invested in your well-being. He cares about every aspect of your life.

But the consequences of worry are even more sinister. Jesus said, "From the heart come evil thoughts, murder, adultery, all sexual immorality, theft, lying, and slander. These are what defile you" (Matthew 15:19–20). We know that these obvious sins corrupt our hearts and lives. But Jesus also said, "Watch out! Don't let your hearts be dulled by carousing and drunkenness, and by the worries of this life" (Luke 21:34). Who knew that our worries were as spiritually damaging to us as "carousing and drunkenness" and the other easy-to-see sins? Who knew that worry dulls our hearts? Jesus knew.

Settle Your Anxiety

Anxiety is related to worry. It's a generalized worry, apprehension, or exaggerated fear that blocks the presence of God in our lives. Jesus warned us that "all too quickly the message is crowded out by the cares and riches and pleasures of this life. And so they never grow into maturity" (Luke 8:14). Bad news! This means that when God is speaking to us, we often don't hear—not because we don't want to listen, but because His voice is drowned out by our anxiety. As a result, we don't grow up in Him the way we should. How sad. We feel justified in holding on to our anxiety because life is scary, but it's that very anxiety that is keeping us from experiencing God in our lives.

Remember that a crowded heart filled with cares, riches, and pleasure can be just as crippled as a hard heart. Jesus said, "Don't let your hearts be troubled. Trust in God, and trust also in me" (John 14:1). According to Jesus, it's our job *not* to let our hearts be troubled. We do that by trusting God, by trusting Jesus. We know that God always does what's best for "those who love God and are called according to his purpose for them" (Romans 8:28). He cares.

Settle Your Anger

While worry and anxiety come from fear, anger comes from a place of pain. It is the animosity we feel when someone or something hurts us. If you hit your thumb with a hammer, stub your toe, or bump your head, your response is predictable. Pain makes us angry, which is why we should be motivated to be unoffendable. The pain of offense leads to anger.

When discussing murder, Jesus said, "But I say, if you are even angry with someone, you are subject to judgment!" (Matthew 5:22). An angry heart is a fertile field for all kinds of acts of animosity, including murder. The psalmist said, "Don't sin by letting anger control you" (Psalm 4:4). Either God will lead your life or anger will mislead your life. It can't be both.

Paul added, "Get rid of all bitterness, rage, anger, harsh words, and slander, as well as all types of evil behavior" (Ephesians 4:31). We know that evil behavior is bad. Anger is also bad because it leads to evil behavior. Angry outbursts are just as serious as bitterness, rage, and slander. We need to stop excusing these damaging behaviors and instead turn to God so He will heal our hurts and brokenness.

Did people in the Bible ever get stressed and angry, or did they write in a vacuum? Their lives were stressful—on average, probably more stressful than ours. We need to stop letting stress, anger, and bitterness control our lives.

154

Settle Your Internal Narrative

Learning to address our negative internal narrative, or story, is a key to heart management. Paul exhorted you to "fix your thoughts on what is true, and honorable, and right, and pure, and lovely, and admirable. Think about things that are excellent and worthy of praise" (Philippians 4:8). I agree. We need to focus our thoughts on the things that build us up, not on our negative interpretation of the unknown and undetermined. We need to stop letting our flawed, broken internal narrative harden our hearts, hurting us and making us angry.

Proverbs tells us that "people with understanding control their anger; a hot temper shows great foolishness" (Proverbs 14:29). Why is a temper, uncontrolled anger, a sign of foolishness? Because "human anger does not produce the righteousness God desires" (James 1:20).

We need to replace our broken internal narratives with God's life-giving narrative for us. If we say that our hearts are good but we are still consumed with fear, anger, worry, or anxiety, we show ourselves to be more clueless than we think. Jesus is commanding us not to fixate on the things that trip up people who are not walking with God.

Jesus said, "So don't worry about these things, saying, 'What will we eat? What will we drink? What will we wear?' These things dominate the thoughts of unbelievers, but your heavenly Father already knows all your needs. Seek the Kingdom of God above all else, and live righteously, and he will give you everything you need" (Matthew 6:31–33).

Here's why we need to shift to God's story, built on His grace and truth. If I were to tell you that I had just destroyed something you love (your pet, your priceless work of art, your car, whatever), and you were convinced that I was telling you the truth, what would your mental and emotional reaction be? I can only imagine.

The emotions you would feel, the thoughts you would think, would be very real, but not very honest. Because they would be based on a lie. I didn't really do it. What difference would the truth make? All the difference in the world! The truth would set you free (John 8:32). Your perceptions, narrative, and heart would be restored.

But what if the things I said were true? Your heart would be under attack. That's where grace would need to kick in. What difference would grace make in your heart over time? Real, unexpected, undeserved grace would heal your heart. It's harder to imagine, and it may not be immediate, but grace would make a difference. Your heart, perceptions, and narrative would be restored. We need to stop thinking like unbelievers and start thinking like Jesus, being full of grace and truth.

THE STORY CONTINUES

Di learned that working with horses often requires leading by example. If we want to settle our horses, we must settle ourselves. We must learn to read their body language and pay attention to our own. We must "settle down, settle down" ourselves so that they can, too.

As humans, we have so many things that can ramp us up, things like fear, worry, anxiety, anger, bitterness, unforgiveness, impatience, grumbling, complaining, jealousy, guilt, shame, regret, false narratives, bad habits, and lack of confidence. All are heart issues and the product of stress caused by living in an unsafe, broken world. Jesus would want us to "settle down, settle down," exchanging our troubled hearts for trust in Him (John 14:1). When we identify and address our heart issues, we free ourselves to partner with God and with others.

Chapter Nine Questions

Question: In which situations or parts of your life do you feel unsafe, out of control, stressed, worried, anxious, or angry?

_____

_____

_____

_____

_____

_____

_____

_____

_____

Question: When was the last time you experienced extreme stress? What was the cause? How exactly did it control your decision-making in the situation?

_____

_____

_____

_____

_____

_____

_____

_____

_____

_____

Question: In the future, how could you let God guard your heart against this recent source of stress?

_____

_____

_____

_____

_____

_____

_____

_____

_____

_____

_____

_____

Action: We must learn to guard our hearts! Create a two-column chart. In the left-hand column, list these specific things you struggle with:

- a fear

- a worry

- a source of anxiety

- a source of anger

- a negative internal narrative

Now, for each thing you listed, find a Bible verse to help you "settle down, settle down" with grace and truth. Record each scripture in the right-hand column and commit at least one of these verses to memory today.

Chapter Nine Notes

_____

_____

_____

_____

_____

_____

_____

_____

_____

_____

_____

_____

_____

_____

_____

Blessed to Bless

REAL STORIES
AMANDA, BOONE, JOSEY, AND DOC

I (Amanda) am so grateful and blessed to have worked with three very different horses during my time with Hearts in Harmony. The experience caused me to look deep within myself and see the parts of me I didn't even know existed. God used each horse to bless me in a different way.

Boone showed me my own stubbornness, my unteachable spirit that I needed to shake off. God blessed me by using Boone as a mirror. He helped me to see deep into my own soul.

Josey was my second horse. When I first met her, she was so downtrodden. That is how I felt when I first started this program. But with a little love and attention, she perked right up. She began to trust me. In time, she would trot alongside me when I ran with her. God blessed me through her warmhearted acceptance.

When I first met Doc, he stomped his feet. He was so excited to work with me. He genuinely wanted to partner with me. He smothered me with love. He showed me how I could approach others. I could be more ready and open. I could have Doc's excitement and acceptance of others when I begin a new relationship. He taught me to assume the best.

Another blessing was when I learned about the difference between being assertive and being aggressive. God used that exercise to show me why I could get aggressive. I had a lot of unforgiveness toward my mom. Facing this truth triggered a process of forgiveness that has enabled me to forgive my mom and learn to love her as she is. That was a huge step for me. Forgiving my mom ended a thirty-seven-year resentment.

I want to thank you all so much. God has blessed me in so many ways through spending time with you and your horses. I will never forget this.

THE BLESSING IS GOD

We were designed by God for blessing: to receive blessing and to give blessing. We are blessed to bless others.

When I was a kid, my parents told me, "It is more blessed to give than to receive" (Acts 20:35). I didn't buy it. To me, being blessed was the feeling you get when you do the right thing. It's a great feeling, but not enough to cause me to put other people first in my life. I didn't buy it because I didn't understand the point. My premise was wrong. Being blessed is far more than a feeling.

How do you define the word *blessed*? What do you think people mean when they wear t-shirts adorned with the single word "Blessed"? Do they wear such shirts because they have a feeling? Because they are enjoying life? Because they are grateful? Or lucky? Or healthy? Or hard-working? Or prosperous? Do they have great cars, houses, boats, vacations, friends, or family? Many people believe that those with the most stuff in this life are the most blessed. Is that even close to right?

To be clear, *blessing* and *prosperity* are not synonymous. According to the Bible, many people prosper without the blessing of God. The psalmist said, "Look at these wicked people—enjoying a life of ease while their riches multiply" (Psalm 73:12). From a biblical perspective, there must be more to being blessed than having wealth and ease.

The word *blessed* can also be translated "happy." [7] But being happy is a feeling. Can a person feel happy without being blessed? Yes. Can a person be blessed without feeling happy? Unfortunately, yes. But blessed people should be the happiest people on the planet.

Here's the short answer. According to what Jesus taught us in His Sermon on the Mount, people who are blessed by God encounter God in many ways. Each beatitude begins with whom will be blessed and finishes with how they will be blessed (Matthew 5:3–10).

Who Is Blessed?

"Those who are poor and realize their need for him..."

"Those who mourn..."

"Those who are humble..."

"Those who hunger and thirst for justice..."

"Those who are merciful..."

"Those whose hearts are pure..."

"Those who work for peace..."

"Those who are persecuted for doing right..."

The blessed people fall into one of two categories. They are either people who desperately need God or people who are walking with God in Christ.

The Fruit of Blessing

"The Kingdom of Heaven is theirs."

"They will be comforted."

"They will inherit the whole earth."

"They will be satisfied."

"They will be shown mercy."

"They will see God."

"They will be called the children of God."

"The Kingdom of Heaven is theirs."

The people blessed by God enter into a relationship with Him. As a result, they receive His will, His comfort, and His mercy. Their souls are satisfied. They become the family of God, and their rewards in life come from God. The fruit of blessing takes many forms. The source of blessing is God Himself. The blessing of God flows from experiencing God. The blessing *is* God, the manifest presence of God, in our lives.

We were made for this. God has had a plan to bless humanity with His presence since He first created us. Our brokenness has not changed the plan. He comes to us in our lowest moments and calls us to faith, which is foundational to our relationship with Him: "It is impossible to please God without faith. Anyone who wants to come to him must believe that God exists and that he rewards those who sincerely seek him" (Hebrews 11:6). When we open our hearts to God and seek Him wholeheartedly, we are blessed as He shows up for us in real, tangible ways.

According to the Apostle Paul, anyone in Jesus can be blessed: "Through Christ Jesus, God has blessed the Gentiles with the same blessing he promised to Abraham, so that we who are believers might receive the promised Holy Spirit through faith" (Galatians 3:14). The *Gentiles* were the people far from God, the spiritual nobodies. Abraham was God's number one spiritual somebody, the father of our faith.

Abraham was God's person of faith who introduced the blessing of God into the world through faith. Everyone in Christ receives Him and the blessing that comes from His presence.

THE BLESSING OF ABRAHAM

God's blessing was promised to Abraham and his descendants, but his descendants may not be who you think. Being a part of Abraham's bloodline doesn't mean that you automatically receive Abraham's blessing. To be a child of Abraham, you must have the faith of Abraham (Romans 9:7–8). That's the critical element: "So the promise is received by faith. It is given as a free gift. And we are all certain to receive it ... if we have faith like Abraham's. For Abraham is the father of all who believe" (Romans 4:16).

Know this: if you are a person of faith, God wants to bless every aspect of your life. He said, "You will experience all these blessings if you obey the LORD your God: Your towns and your fields will be blessed. Your children and your crops will be blessed. The offspring of your herds and flocks will be blessed. Your fruit baskets and breadboards will be blessed. Wherever you go and whatever you do, you will be blessed" (Deuteronomy 28:2–6). This may be hard to believe and fully comprehend, but yes, God wants to share life with you. He wants to be a part of every area of your life.

The blessing of Abraham is given to people of faith "so that we who are believers might receive the promised Holy Spirit through faith" (Galatians 3:14). God's gift of His Holy

Spirit is the source from which the blessing of God flows. The blessing of God is God.

But to what end? Why did God bless Abraham and his family of faith with the Holy Spirit? There's a single reason: God promised Abraham that he would be a blessing to every tribe, tongue, people, and nation through his countless descendants (Genesis 12:2–3). God blesses people of faith so that they can be a blessing to others. This has been God's plan all along. We are blessed to bless.

BE FILLED TO OVERFLOWING

We should all be in awe of God. He has created us to have His Holy Spirit dwell in our hearts through faith, filling us to overflowing with His presence. We're not just talking about the warm, fuzzy feeling some people get when they sense the presence of God in their lives. We are talking about the blessing of God Himself taking up residence in our hearts.

Jesus said, "Anyone who believes in me may come and drink! For the Scriptures declare, 'Rivers of living water will flow from his heart'" (John 7:38). John further explained, "When he said 'living water,' he was speaking of the Spirit, who would be given to everyone believing in him" (John 7:39).

What does it look like when someone receives the Holy Spirit of God? It looks like a spiritual nobody becoming a spiritual somebody in Jesus! On the day of Pentecost, Peter quoted the prophet Joel: "'In the last days,' God says, 'I will pour out my Spirit upon all people. ... In those days I will pour out my Spirit even on my servants—men and women alike—and they will prophesy'" (Acts 2:17–18). That includes the Gentiles, the people far from God! All the spiritual nobodies get to be blessed by God and embraced as spiritual somebodies.

God doesn't pour out His Spirit sparingly. No, He has chosen to pour out His Spirit on us to the point of overflowing! Why? Maybe it's because in our brokenness, we tend to leak. But our God is more than enough.

Paul said, "Don't be drunk with wine, because that will ruin your life. Instead, be filled with the Holy Spirit" (Ephesians 5:18). In New Testament Greek, the present tense implies an ongoing, continual action, [8] so a more literal translation would read, "Be *being* filled with the Holy Spirit." We are continually in the process of being filled to overflowing with the manifest presence of God.

Jesus said, "I will ask the Father, and he will give you another Advocate, who will never leave you. He is the Holy Spirit, who leads into all truth. The world cannot receive him, because it isn't looking for him and doesn't recognize him. But you know him, because he lives with you now and later will be in you" (John 14:16–17). God's Advocate, the Holy Spirit, is with us. He is for us. He is on our side. He speaks into our lives as our counselor, comforter, encourager, shepherd, and friend.

My concern is that you may be satisfied with experiencing the presence of God *with* you and not realize that there's more. Perhaps you have experienced Him through others but not *in you*. That's not enough. When you are truly blessed, you personally experience the Spirit of God in you. That is God's plan of blessing. Otherwise, you are still an outsider looking in. Jesus is inviting you into the family: "For his Spirit joins with our spirit to affirm that we are God's children" (Romans 8:16).

OVERFLOWING GENEROSITY

Different people may give you different information about how you can know if you have received the Holy Spirit. The clear evidence is a new-found generosity, the God-given ability to be strong for the weak. It is something that comes from deep inside you, but it's more than a feeling. It's an outward expression that you have "died to this life, and your real life is hidden with Christ in God" (Colossians 3:3). This is what you see in the New Testament story. When people received the Holy Spirit, they became remarkably generous.

Lydia was an affluent, influential businesswoman. When she believed, she was baptized, and so were all the people in her sphere of influence. Then she was eager to demonstrate the fruit of her new-found faith and relationship with God through her overflowing generosity: "'If you agree that I am a true believer in the Lord,' she said, 'come and stay at my home.' And she urged us until we agreed" (Acts 16:15).

Later in the same chapter, Paul and his team were arrested and beaten in Philippi. There was an earthquake that made it possible for them to escape, but they chose not to. Paul and his companions stayed back and led the jailer to faith. He

171

became a different man, a surprisingly generous man: "The jailer cared for them and washed their wounds. Then he and everyone in his household were immediately baptized. He brought them into his house and set a meal before them, and he and his entire household rejoiced because they all believed in God" (Acts 16:33–34).

When the jailer received Christ and the Holy Spirit, it changed him. In that day, jailers were not known for caring for their prisoners or inviting them into their homes. The jailer was blessed by God and instantly became a blessing to others. His new-found generosity overflowed.

When we receive the Holy Spirit on the inside, there is spiritual fruit that becomes evident on the outside, including "love, joy, peace, patience, kindness, goodness, faithfulness, gentleness, and self-control" (Galatians 5:22–23). If you were marooned on a desert island, this fruit of the Holy Spirit would be of little use to you. The fruit of the Spirit is not for you. It's given so you can be a blessing to others. The fruit of the Spirit is God's presence in your life overflowing into the lives of those around you.

The gifts of the Spirit, like the fruit of the Spirit, are about the presence of God flowing through you to others. Paul said, "For I long to visit you so I can bring you some spiritual gift that will help you grow strong in the Lord" (Romans 1:11). The gifts of the Spirit are all about encouraging and blessing others with the blessings we have received from God.

BE STRONG FOR THE WEAK

In other words, God blesses us so we can be a blessing to others, specifically those who need it most. We are to be strong for the weak and for those who are walking with God (Matthew 5:3–10), including: "those who are poor and realize their need for him," "those who mourn," "those who are humble," "those who hunger and thirst for justice," "those who are merciful," "those whose hearts are pure," "those who work for peace," and "those who are persecuted for doing right."

In my family of origin, being a family member meant that you were held to a higher standard than others. Maybe that example helps to explain why Jesus had such a strained relationship with the religious leaders of His day. It's possible that He was especially stern with them because they were supposed to be the ones pointing the way to God for other people. Maybe He had higher expectations for the Pharisees, Sadducees, and teachers of the Law than they had for themselves.

They were meant to be the shepherds of Israel. Their role and training gave them more understanding of God and more access to the Spirit of God. Sadly, they were totally missing the blessing of God: "Yet they [the religious leaders] shamelessly cheat widows out of their property and then pretend to be pious by making long prayers in public" (Mark 12:40).

It's not hard to see why their behavior infuriated Jesus. At some point, His mom became a widow. He and His siblings were raised fatherless, as second-class citizens. When the shepherds of Israel cheated widows, Jesus took it personally. Their false piety sickened Him. Maybe that's why His brother James spoke so strongly on the topic as well: "Pure and genuine religion in the sight of God the Father means caring for orphans and widows in their distress and refusing to let the world corrupt you" (James 1:27).

How many of us would acknowledge that it's important for people of faith to be strong for the weak? Let me ask the question another way: How many of us think that tithing is no longer important? Some see it as an unnecessary, outdated remnant of the Old Covenant. The tithe was to be used to help support "the Levites, ... the foreigners living among you, the orphans, and the widows.... Then the LORD your God will bless you in all your work" (Deuteronomy 14:29). Moses taught us not to cut corners when helping the disadvantaged. The tithe was given so we could be strong for the weak and for those who are walking with God.

Jesus quoted the Law when He said, "You will always have the poor among you" (Matthew 26:11). The Law goes on to say, "That is why I am commanding you to share freely with the poor" (Deuteronomy 15:11). We are blessed when we take our responsibility to be strong for the weak seriously, but "cursed is anyone who denies justice to foreigners, orphans, or widows" (Deuteronomy 27:19). Being cursed is the exact opposite of being blessed. God will withhold His blessing from us if we are not generous with those who need it most.

Jesus was also the one who said, "It is more blessed to give than to receive" (Acts 20:35). Our parents did not make up generosity to teach us to be more sharing and caring. It was Jesus. He was not talking about the feeling we have when we do the right thing. He was talking about the amazing reality that God is the single source of our blessings. He shows up for us in real, tangible ways and pours His Spirit into our hearts. He reveals Himself to us so we can personally receive and share His presence and provision with others. Yes, when God shows up, we are blessed. But we are *more* blessed when we share His presence with others.

THE STORY CONTINUES

In all the ways described in this book, having a relationship with Jesus Christ and with His community matters. Jesus "gave his life to free us from every kind of sin, to cleanse us, and to make us his very own people, totally committed to doing good deeds" (Titus 2:14). This was His mission. Now it's ours. Without Christ, we are disconnected from God, the One who made us and loves us. Jesus came to live among us. He humbled Himself and entered our broken world to connect us with God.

Jesus challenges each of us to "come and see" (John 1:39), to give His life and teaching honest consideration. As we get to know Him, He invites us to follow Him. This was and is His open, universal invitation. Our brokenness keeps us from God. We are hard-hearted and clueless. Jesus came, lived, and died to overcome the barrier of our brokenness and sin and to bring us back into relationship with Him and His heavenly Father.

Jesus gives each of us a choice: to believe or not to believe, to receive or not to receive. Our response to the grace of God shapes our present life and eternal destiny. His open heart to us is called *grace*. Our open heart to Him is called *faith*. It is by faith and grace alone that we can experience new life in Christ.

God designed life-change (*repentance*) to happen through relationships—a relationship with Him and relationships with each other. Jesus calls us to be part of His family and to find our place in His community, His Church. God loves us and is calling us to walk in real, honest, open-hearted relationship with Him and with each other. He has so much more for us than we realize.

Without following Jesus, we'll never become the people God created us to be. We are designed to learn by following. Jesus said, "Anyone who wants to serve me must follow me" (John 12:26). It's not what we do *for* Jesus that matters. It's what we do *in* Jesus and *with* Jesus that matters. We must follow Jesus. We must walk with Jesus. We must partner with Jesus. We must "be found in him, not having a righteousness of [our] own that comes from the law, but that which is through faith in Christ—the righteousness that comes from God on the basis of faith" (Philippians 3:9 NIV).

Chapter Ten Questions

Question: What are some of the ways God is pouring blessing into your life now?

_____

_____

_____

_____

_____

_____

_____

_____

_____

_____

Question: How are you allowing God's generosity to overflow from you to others? What blessings are you receiving from God but holding back from others?

_____

_____

_____

_____

_____

_____

_____

_____

_____

_____

Question: What is one way God has blessed you with strength where others you know are weak? How, specifically, can you be strong for others' weakness in this area?

_____

_____

_____

_____

_____

_____

_____

_____

_____

_____

_____

_____

Action: List all the ways you can think of in which God showed up for you in the past month. Then think of someone who may need you to show up for him or her this coming week. Pray for God to fill you to overflowing so you can overflow to the person who needs to experience the love of Jesus through you.

Chapter Ten Notes

_____

_____

_____

_____

_____

_____

_____

_____

_____

_____

_____

_____

_____

_____

_____

_____

About the Author

VAN FIELDEN has served as a pastor and bi-vocational church planter over the past forty-four years. For the most recent twenty-two years, he was the lead pastor of Vista Church in Orlando, Florida, a multicultural, multigenerational church with a diverse congregation. People far from God grow and learn side by side with mature leaders from mission organizations like Cru (Campus

Crusade for Christ), Wycliffe, Pioneers, Missionary Ventures, and World Team. Today, he is the spiritual leader and teacher for Hearts in Harmony, a nonprofit ministry that creates an amazing environment in which horses help humans to find hope, healing, and transformation.

About Dark Horse Horsemanship and Hearts in Harmony

Dark Horse Horsemanship is a family-friendly facility that focuses on natural horsemanship and foundation training. We seek to help people explore their potential through the art of horsemanship and to provide a non-judgmental environment where they can learn, grow, reach attainable goals, and prove themselves. As a full-service facility, we offer individual and group lessons, workshops, training, boarding, and more.

Hearts in Harmony is a non-profit organization dedicated to human transformation through equine-assisted learning. Horses are brilliant instructors. They give honest feedback with no judgment or ego. They respond positively or negatively according to the person's body language and internal energy.

At Hearts in Harmony, horses are the catalyst for helping people challenge their perspectives and accelerate personal and relational growth. Through the powerful horse–human connection, participants' emotional scars may begin to heal and new life skills develop. Our programs provide opportunities for heart change, positive and productive social interaction, improved academic performance, and improved cognitive functioning.

Horses help change lives, develop stronger individuals, and build stronger communities. We currently serve foster children, youth at risk, men and women in recovery, veterans, first responders, and their families. We offer one-on-one counseling, learning opportunities for home schoolers, and an internship program for local university students.

We invite you to be a part of the change!

Follow, donate, volunteer, and/or inquire today at DarkHorseEquestrian.com.

About Renown Publishing

Renown Publishing was founded with one mission in mind: to make your great idea famous.

At Renown Publishing, we don't just publish. We work hard to pair strategy with innovative marketing techniques so that your book launch is the start of something bigger.

Learn more at RenownPublishing.com.

REFERENCES

Notes

1. Richardson, Don. *Peace Child*. Baker Publishing Group, 2005.

2. Richardson, Don. *Eternity in Their Hearts*. Baker Publishing Group, 2006.

3. Office of Mental Health and Suicide Prevention. "2021 National Veteran Suicide Prevention Annual Report." U. S. Department of Veterans Affairs. 2021. https://www.mentalhealth.va.gov/docs/data-sheets/2021/2021-National-Veteran-Suicide-Prevention-Annual-Report-FINAL-9-8-21.pdf.

4. Blue Letter Bible, "Strong's G2842 – *koinonia*." https://www.blueletterbible.org/lexicon/g2842/kjv/tr/0-1/.

5. Brodie, Jessica. "What Every Christian Needs to Know About Koinonia." Crosswalk.com. April 25, 2022. https://www.crosswalk.com/faith/spiritual-life/what-every-christian-needs-to-know-about-koinonia.html.

6. Lexico, "prodigal." https://www.lexico.com/en/definition/prodigal.

7. Blue Letter Bible, "Strong's G3107 – *Makarios*." https://www.blueletterbible.org/lexicon/g3107/kjv/tr/0-1/.

8. Keating, Corey. "Greek Verb Tenses (Intermediate Discussion)." NTGreek.org. https://www.ntgreek.org/learn_nt_greek/inter-tense.htm.

Made in the USA
Columbia, SC
20 March 2023

14003632R00111